Upon Her Shoulders

Upon Her Shoulders

Southeastern Native Women
Share Their Stories of
Justice, Spirit, and Community

MARY ANN JACOBS
CHERRY MAYNOR BEASLEY
ULRIKE WIETHAUS
EDITORS

BLAIR

Printed in the United States of America
Cover design by Callie Riek. Cover art by Jessica Clark, Lumbee,
Lumbee Pinecone II. Interior design by April Leidig.

Blair is an imprint of Carolina Wren Press.

*The mission of Blair/Carolina Wren Press is to seek out, nurture, and
promote literary work by new and historically neglected writers.*

We gratefully acknowledge the ongoing support
of general operations by the Durham Arts Council's
United Arts Fund and the North Carolina Arts Council.

Library of Congress Cataloging-in-Publication Data
Names: Jacobs, Mary Ann, editor. | Beasley, Cherry Maynor, 1951– editor. |
    Wiethaus, Ulrike, editor. | Titla, Mary Kim, writer of foreword.
Title: Upon her shoulders : Southeastern Native women share their stories of
    justice, spirit, and community / Mary Ann Jacobs, Cherry Maynor Beasley,
    and Ulrike Wiethaus, editors.
Description: [Durham, North Carolina] : Blair, [2022] | Includes bibliographical
    references.
Identifiers: LCCN 2022003108 (print) | LCCN 2022003109 (ebook) |
    ISBN 9781949467802 (paperback) | ISBN 9781949467819 (ebook)
Subjects: LCSH: Indian women—Southern States—Biography. | Indian women—
    Southern States—Social conditions—21st century. | American literature—
    Women authors. | American literature—Indian authors. | Literature, Modern—
    21st century. | Poetry, Modern—21st century. | LCGFT: Autobiographies. |
    Poetry.
Classification: LCC PS508.I5 U66 2022 (print) | LCC PS508.I5 (ebook) |
    DDC 810.8/0928708997075 [B]—dc23/eng/20220314
LC record available at https://lccn.loc.gov/2022003108
LC ebook record available at https://lccn.loc.gov/2022003109

This volume is dedicated to Ms. Rosa Winfree, Ms. Ruth Revels, and Ms. Barbara Locklear who carried the hope that started it all.

Contents

Part Two · Spirit Medicine

Part Three • Getting Justice When There Was None

Foreword

MARY KIM TITLA

Imagine spending twenty years as a TV news reporter. That was me—the first Native American to do so in the Grand Canyon state. I would often reference myself as a modern-day Apache storyteller. It was a source of pride to come from a lineage of storytellers. My grandparents and my parents were and are wonderful storytellers. I recall as a child sitting next to a campfire on the San Carlos Apache Reservation listening to my grandma Gussie telling stories about her childhood and my father Phillip telling stories about Coyote, the trickster. Growing up poor, we did not have electricity for a big part of my childhood, and thus no television, so storytelling time is a cherished memory. The downside? I procrastinated as an adult telling myself, "One day I will video record my grandmother while she's still alive." Unfortunately, I never did, and I regret it to this day.

The compilation of life stories and poetry in this book is simply superb and serves as a model to generations of women who wished they had captured the stories, perspectives, and folklore of generations past. The inclusion of writings from both elders and young women helps bring balance to life perspectives and validate that while the writers may be generations apart, their words of love for their people, their families, and their lifeways are harmonious.

Reading the contributions of these amazing writers recalled the commonalities among Native women across the U.S. I can speak to this because I am now a grandmother and I have had the privilege of traveling to many tribal communities where I have witnessed this to be true. Historically, Native women are cherished figures who not only held leadership roles, they also played major roles in the family and in their villages as providers, educators, counselors, advocates, visionaries, and spiritual leaders. The Lumbee tribal community certainly has its treasury of women trailblazers.

One of those women is a longtime beloved educator and esteemed community leader, Rosa Winfree. In July of 1981, at her invitation, I traveled to Pembroke, North Carolina, to attend the Lumbee Homecoming. That year I carried the title of Miss National Congress of American Indians (NCAI), which allowed me to serve as a national ambassador for American Indian tribes for a one-year period. It was my first time traveling to North Carolina, let alone to the Lumbee tribal community. I knew very little about the Lumbee people or the land they called home. While there, and this is something I will never forget, Ms. Rosa and her husband, Frank, took me on a grand tour of the area. Ms. Rosa proudly pointed out and explained significant and historical tribal sites.

I learned a lot that day about the resiliency of the Lumbee people and specifically Lumbee women. Like most tribal people, they are deeply connected spiritually and culturally to the land and its elements. The Lumbee Tribe takes pride in its origin, history, and lifeways. Hunting and farming are at the heart of their survival story. One stop I will always remember was at a tobacco farm, mainly because I had never seen one, or a tobacco plant for that matter. I thought it so significant. I asked if I could take a tobacco leaf home with me. I pressed it into a book and kept it as a keepsake for many years.

Another memory is my first taste of delicious southern food. Lumbee women can surely cook up any southern dish with their own cultural ingredients. During Lumbee Homecoming, delicious southern food is everywhere you turn. I discovered my love for grits, barbecued pork, and sweet tea, although I had to dilute the tea a bit. While the land, with its beautiful pine trees, the tasty southern food, and the lush tobacco farms left a wonderful impression on me, it was the heartfelt hospitality of the Lumbee people and the loving embrace of the Winfree family that I will remember most.

Reading the poems and stories in this book allows readers to travel back and forth in time, to the cherished childhood days of the elders and to the modern-day experiences of Lumbee youth. I am especially grateful for the insights provided by Rosa Winfree, who remained a dear friend and served as one of my mentors after my first trip to North Carolina.

I will end with a unique story about my grandma Gussie. While I did not video record her life story, my father was able to capture on paper a special encounter she had as a child. One day a young bear cub visited Gussie's family encampment. When she saw the bear cub, she thought it was a dog, as she had never seen a bear. She was not afraid of the bear cub, and it did not seem too afraid of her. When her family saw her playing with the bear cub, they screamed at her to get away, fearing mother bear might be nearby. The cub ran away. Weeks went by, and to Gussie's delight, the bear cub appeared once again. With glee, and without anyone noticing, she left to play with the little bear. This happened more than once. When winter hit, the visits abruptly ended. Gussie and her family also moved away. She never saw her friend the bear again. My grandmother had long beautiful hair, which did not gray very much when she became an old woman. The bear is considered a sacred animal to the Apache people. Many believe the bear blessed her with a long life and dark hair. Cherish all who bless you with their stories.

Preface

. . . .

Women Sharing Their Wisdom

MARY ANN JACOBS
CHERRY MAYNOR BEASLEY
ULRIKE WIETHAUS

THE POWER OF STORY

This is a book of Southeastern American Indian women's stories and poems. Telling stories and listening to stories in a communal American Indian women's context: this is how stories and poems become empowering. Entering a relationship with the storyteller and poet, the listeners live both in the here and now and in the realm of the story and poem. A storytelling, whether as prose or poem, takes place not once, but twice. The storyteller/poet and her audience experience a story or poem in two places simultaneously: the physical space we inhabit as embodied beings in the present moment and the space of our imaginations, of our memory, and of the knowledge and wisdom to which the story and the poem carry us. In locally well-known stories, the space of the story's content and the space of the telling often overlap. To tell a story in the place of the story's origin engages all of what we are now: our senses, our feeling of being in the world as who we truly are, and our discernment. This story or poem happened here where you were born, here where you live now, here near this river and these fields, here in these woods, here at the corner of that street. Traditionally, an American Indian telling of stories took place in a finely tuned combination of the right time, the right place, the right storyteller, the right audience, and the right words. We hope that our readers will pick up the book and find a story and a poem at the time and the place that is right for them.

Frequently, when Southeastern American Indian women gather to work, raise children, care for family members, collect and prepare food, participate in economic development, create art and home aesthetics, and worship and address community concerns and needs, they also always share their experiences and knowledge. Such sharing is most often indirect. Two common examples of indirect ways of sharing are the telling of stories and parables. When women gather in joint activities, it is common to hear, "Do you remember when . . ." or "Tell me again about the time when . . ." When a question arises, the response is often, "Well, do you remember your Aunt Mary, when she . . ." or "Let me tell you about a lady I knew." The power of these forms of communication is that they allow the hearer to understand the full context of shared knowledge and to decide if the example shared fits her own needs. This type of communication also maintains relationships that are "horizontal" and egalitarian rather than "vertical" and hierarchical.

Stories are also easy to remember. Which of us has not heard a young child point out a part of the bedtime story we inadvertently skipped? Stories also allow for a sharing of emotions that tend to be neglected in vertical patterns of communication that rely on abstracted and thus diminished facts and unilateral directions and advice.

It is with this recognition of the power of the story that the three editors designed this book. This edited volume succeeds a previous collection of essays on the same topic, but from a Western scholarly perspective. *American Indian Women of Proud Nations: Essays on History, Language, and Education*, published in 2016, is a collection of scholarly articles designed to provide academic insights into the lived experiences of contemporary American Indian women. While many of the collection's scholarly articles relied on the gathering and analysis of women's stories, they presented an academic researcher's understanding of shared stories. In this volume, we have chosen instead to provide the reader with the experience of participating directly in the lives of women beyond the lens of Western scholarship. We have gathered their stories, whether presented in prose or poetic format, over several years. We have reflected on them, talked about them, and applied their inherent knowledge and wisdom when appropriate in our own lives. As editors, we chose to group the stories according to three overlapping themes: community, spirituality, and justice. We also added reflection questions and suggestions to access some of the stories' deeper layers, perhaps even their hidden meanings. By no means are these questions and suggestions comprehensive. They are only guideposts along the way.

. . . .

This volume builds on yet another layer of lived community. The three editors have helped design intentional experiences at Indigenous conferences both in the Southeast and internationally. Our goal was to expand the environment in which American

Indian and Indigenous women from diverse tribal and First Nations communities and across the life cycle can share their experiences and hard-won wisdom through stories. We designed and presented numerous workshops to facilitate a story's communicatory goal of horizontal sharing and reflecting. Frequently, we designated a wall where women could post their thoughts and share their words of wisdom at any time during and after a workshop. Whether at a workshop or during a shared meal, an honoring ceremony, or talking circle afterward, we observed women choosing to write and post their insights on note cards to share with other women. During conference breaks, women would go to the wall and read the comments, often adding words of agreement, such as *Amen*. As editors, we have collected the communal wall notes over the years, and we share some of them in this volume at the end of each section under the title "In Closing: Contemplating Words of Wisdom by Women Elders." We invite you to share your words of wisdom with your own community. We hope that as you work through each section and reflect on the stories, you will record (through prose, songs, or poems) your newly gained insights. We hope you will find others to share these with and in turn will invite their thoughts. Perhaps you will record and share your own stories and those of your family and community.

THE CONTRIBUTORS

The women authors featured in this volume sustained connections of some kind or another with the American Indian Women of Proud Nations (AIWPN) organization over many years. Many of the women who gifted their written stories or told us their stories in interviews for the volume offered conference talks or workshops for an AIWPN conference at some point in the past or were deeply involved in the planning and implementation of one or more of the AIWPN conferences. Some of their poems first appeared in the AIWPN conference programs.

Throughout their lives, they have put in the hard work of uplifting American Indian women, girls, and families through poetry, art, music, education, storytelling, life coaching, tribal representation, nonprofit leadership, health careers, and entrepreneurship. Most of our contributors have grown up in American Indian communities, and many still live in their tribal homelands. They maintain their ties in many ways, including their connection to the AIWPN initiative.

Some of the women featured in this volume have passed on. We believe their stories and poetry may be the only written record that we have left of their vital impact on Southeastern American Indian people and communities. Some of the storytellers are very young. They are just beginning to build their lives and careers, yet their stories and poetry are evidence of their desire to "make themselves useful" and to give back to their communities. Other contributors are elders in their communities, not so much because of their age, but because of their long and steadfast careers in service to their people, where they find a way to positively impact the American Indian and Indigenous people they encounter.

Most of the women gathered in this volume live in or have grown up in American Indian communities. They make a point to maintain ties to their own tribal communities in many ways and intertribally and regionally in their connection to AIWPN. We are grateful to all the women featured in this volume. Some of their stories were collected before the publication of our first co-edited volume of scholarly conference essays in 2016, and the authors have been very patient waiting for their stories to be published here. Our collection is a testimony to our authors' wisdom, courage, and faith in our multiyear project. As editors, we are grateful for their many gifts and honored to present their written work. While the editors have chosen to present these powerful stories in three distinct sections, each story and each poem in and of itself contains the themes of all three sections. Each author was given the gift of many talents and answered the call to be "useful." Likewise, each confronted social injustices or fought for social justice for herself, her family, and community, and for the world into which the Creator placed them. Finally, nearly every author shared openly that their spirit and spirit connection provided them with the ability to move forward continuously. It is the editors' hope that the reader will find the three dimensions in their own story as well.

BACKGROUND OF THE AIWPN PROJECT

Both of our volumes grew from the vision for an annual American Indian women's conference of three Lumbee women elders: Rosa Revels Winfree, Ruth Revels, and Barbara Locklear. These elders contributed their own stories to the collection in this book. Together with one of the editors, Ulrike Wiethaus, they convened the first conference at Wake Forest University in 2007. Other North Carolina universities such as the University of North Carolina at Pembroke, Western Carolina University (with strong support from the Eastern Band of Cherokee Indians), and the University of North Carolina at Chapel Hill followed suit.

The Haliwa-Saponi and Coharie tribal nations hosted the conference in subsequent years. The conference mission has been to "support American Indian women's efforts to build healthier lives for themselves, their families, and their communities in a spirit of holistic inquiry and empowerment." In our first volume of this two-volume project, we worked in the spirit of the mission statement by collecting keynote addresses and presentations by invited speakers, all of whom were well-established American Indian Studies and Western scholars in their respective fields. Their essays cover themes such as tribal history with a special emphasis on Native women in the Southeast, language revitalization efforts and the narrative knowledge inherent in Indigenous oral culture, and traditional educational systems in the context of the ongoing colonization of American Indian educational practices and values.

The first book named women's experiences of historical trauma and their ongoing efforts to preserve and rebuild their Native nations. The second volume follows closely the vision of the American Indian Women of Proud Nation's conference, namely "to incorporate Indigenous cultural traditions, language, history, and values to build intergenerational relationships and to develop a movement-building framework for collaborative leadership in five vital areas: education, community, health, spirituality, and economic development" (taken from the AIWPN website). Whereas the first volume presented American Indian and non-Native women scholars, the second volume gathers the voices of American Indian women elders and younger women who participated in the conferences by attending or giving workshops, contributed to story circles, organized honoring ceremonies for elders and children, and shared their poetry and artwork. Rather than sharing their knowledge through scholarship, the authors of this volume offer contemplative reflections of American Indian women's lived experiences, all in the form of autobiographical vignettes and poems. By "contemplative reflections," we mean the cultivation of a "deepened awareness, concentration, and insight."[1] Following Tobin Hart, we agree that "inviting the contemplative [mode] simply includes the natural human capacity for knowing through silence, looking inward, pondering deeply, beholding, witnessing the contents of our consciousness."[2]

In her wide-ranging study *Selu: Seeking the Corn-Mother's Wisdom*, non-enrolled Cherokee/Appalachian writer Marilou Awiakta offers her understanding of an American Indian contemplative approach to story and poetry as follows.

> First, we settle quietly into common ground. Then we go to the heart of the matter—the definition, or "being"—of the story. From there we spin strands of thought outward and in ever-widening circles to a parameter of understanding, where the story itself can be told. In short, we follow the pattern of the Native American story and weave a web where we can be still and *know* that in the belly of the story is life for us all.[3]

The authors whose stories are collected here teach through autobiographical example. Their stories and poems are the result

1. Chick, "Mindfulness in the Classroom."
2. Hart, "Opening the Contemplative Mind," 31.
3. Awiakta, *Selu*, 155.

of contemplating lives lived well. In turn, they invite contemplation of our own commitments to the three domains of this book: community, spirituality, and justice.

FURTHER READING

American Indian Women of Proud Nations. https://aiwpn.org/. Accessed December 21, 2020.

Awiakta, Marilou. *Selu: Seeking the Corn-Mother's Wisdom.* Golden, CO: Fulcrum, 1993.

Beasley, Cherry Maynor, Mary Ann Jacobs, and Ulrike Wiethaus, eds. *American Indian Women of Proud Nations: Essays on History, Language, and Education.* New York: Peter Lang Publishing, 2016.

Bruchac, Joseph. *our stories remember: American Indian History, Culture, and Values through Storytelling.* Golden, CO: Fulcrum 2003.

Chick, Nancy. "Mindfulness in the Classroom." https://cft.vanderbilt.edu/guides-sub-pages/contemplative-pedagogy/. Accessed November 15, 2020.

Eder, Donna, Regina Holyan, and Gregory Cajete. *Life Lessons through Storytelling: Children's Exploration of Ethics.* Bloomington: Indiana University Press, 2010.

Harjo, Joy, and Gloria Bird. *Reinventing the Enemy's Language: Contemporary Native Women's Writings of North America.* New York: W. W. Norton, 1997.

Hart, Tobin. "Opening the Contemplative Mind in the Classroom." *Journal of Transformative Education*, 2, no. 1 (January 2004): 28–46.

Mihesuah, Devon Abbott. *Indigenous American Women: Decolonization, Empowerment, Activism.* Lincoln: University of Nebraska Press, 2003.

. . . .

PART ONE

Make Yourself Useful, Child

Cherry Maynor Beasley

Introduction

Indigenous people in the Americas are not one cultural group but many. What they share, however, is a repeated threat to their social systems caused by colonial invasion, historical inaccuracies, policies of genocide and forced assimilation, and limited opportunities. Alex Wilson has developed a model for American Indian identity that addresses the complexity of identities. Wilson notes that all aspects of identity are interrelated.

Social and family structures differ among tribal communities. They also change over time to assure continued survival by the tribe, most often referred to as "our people." For most Indigenous people, the basic unit of organization is the family. Family structures extend beyond the nuclear family, most often including members of the extended family (aunts, uncles, cousins) as well as people who are not related by blood but by relationship. These family units organize and maintain the activities needed to sustain the group. These include food preparation, child rearing, and all aspects of economic well-being. The extended family unit provides the child with a structure through which to understand her role in the world and cosmos. Indigenous communities value responsibility; the extended family structure provides the opportunity for all to have some role.

All social groups live in distinct cultural systems. As is true for men, a cultural system aids women in developing a pattern of relationships and sense of belonging. It helps women to develop purpose, to explore roles, and to define opportunities. Cultural groups teach their members norms of social behavior through observation of family and community. In addition, they transmit knowledge about a community's origin, tribal and family stories, attitudes toward the people, the land and nature, and tribal sovereignty. Social belonging increases resilience and security.

The community-based development of identity is a journey throughout life. It begins in early childhood, providing a foundation on which one builds through the years. This section provides the reader with a glimpse into how, as young children, Southeastern Native women were provided with a sense of belonging that included an active role in the family or community groups ("making yourself useful"). Each woman used this strong sense of identity to progress through life. We see the women contributing to the family and community at an early age. When life's opportunities challenged them, they expanded their range of activities and embraced change. They fearlessly embraced new opportunities that often initially presented as hardships to learn and create a new role for themselves.

The stories, most of them by elders who review a long life lived in community and usefulness, demonstrate that the social value of offering young girls a strong sense of "being useful" was not only available during their early years but throughout their lives. The women we encounter in these pages embrace the idea and philosophy of "make yourself useful, child" as a life journey.

Intentionally seizing life's opportunities to be useful, Indigenous women are learning from these and then holding a space for others.

In her poem "My Questions for Creator," Madison York, a young Eastern Band of Cherokee woman, describes her preparation for a career in the medical profession. As she makes her choice, she struggles to integrate physical, emotional, social, and spiritual dimensions of her life. These include the pervasive racism that attempts to cage her into stereotypical "Native" looks and the resulting disbelief when she does not fulfill racist expectations; her discovery of an "endless mind" that knows no limits and that, unlike racism, can range far and wide; her acceptance of the gift of a healer's heart "so large it could hold the universe." Finally, the poem maps Madison's reconciliation of the Creator's gifts to her and the challenges of her "walk in two worlds," Native and non-Native.

Ruth Revels provides us a look into the desire to go to school, "to be busy" acting out the things she read in books. In her story, we see a glimpse of the role her mother had in providing her with opportunities for an education. Her realization of the limited opportunities in a segregated social structure would force her and her family to leave the Lumbee community. Ruth Revels (in the Lumbee pattern of communication, "Ms. Ruth") made herself useful as an educator, executive director of an urban American Indian organization, and then as a leader in the North Carolina Commission of Indian Affairs. A member of the Lumbee Tribe, she and her husband were among the founding members of the Guilford Native American Association, an urban center for American Indians from many different tribes in Greensboro, North Carolina. Ms. Ruth selected the Guilford Native American Association's art gallery as the site for sharing her story, a peaceful place filled with art from various tribes. Ms. Ruth explained why she selected the location: "I wanted you to see our place. And it will give you a good idea of our people." The conversation was long but low-key, punctuated often by people who came by "to just speak to Ms. Ruth." For the last two years of her life, Ms. Ruth devoted her talents to being the chair of the North Carolina Indian Commission. As chair, she participated in the annual three-day-long Indian Unity Conference. During that conference, Cherry briefly talked to Ms. Ruth. She looked forward to continuing her work on education, social justice, and the economic and spiritual well-being of Indian people, as well as educating others about who we are. Ms. Ruth passed away a day after the conference concluded.

Mary Ann Elliott presents the reader with the opportunity to view life when one is part of two social systems. A child of a southern white mother and southern Tuscarora Indian father, Mary Ann Elliott grew up in the segregated South, half white and half Indian on a farm in an area that was settled primarily by Lumbee. She recounts living in poverty where even the children had jobs. The family moved from a primarily Indian community to a city where employers were "hiring any able-bodied worker they could get to move into the area." In the city were springing up communities of families who had not lived far from agricultural societies but had moved to the city to become blue-collar workers. Dr. Elliott takes us on a journey of facing one obstacle to the next, but "hard work" and having "pride in what they did" has been key to her success. She points out key lessons learned as she progressed from poverty through working as a woman in a predominantly male profession to becoming an advocate for others.

Mary Alice Pinchbeck Teets learned at an early age that music provided her a means to be useful. She shares the important role that family and community had in encouraging her to embrace her talents and share them with the community. Like other Native women, adversity forced her to leave her tribal community and family to obtain work. She sought opportunities to "come back home" to teach. She made herself useful as an educator, educational administrator, music director, and community advocate. Mary Alice began her story with pointing out some of her memorabilia and prized possessions that mattered to her: several antique organs; pictures of family, peers, and her students; and newspaper articles. The memorabilia included photos of another woman. Esther Maynor was little known in the community, yet Mary Alice noted, "I just admire what she did. She started out with nothing but made a way for herself. In her will, she gave her money to the University of North Carolina at Pembroke so the Honors College could be started." As this example demonstrates, Mary Alice is still making herself useful by collecting memorabilia so the community does not lose its collective memory.

Barbara Locklear shares a detailed story of growing up poor and starting life by making herself useful to her family of origin, her own immediate family, and her business. As an elder, she also is passionate about sharing her views of how to find one's way and keep on it despite setbacks. Ms. Barbara had a drive to teach, to be an artist, and to work with others. Ms. Barbara reminds us of the need to follow one's inner voice even when the way is not clear. Her thirst for knowledge and the arts caused her to embrace more deeply those areas in which she had already developed some expertise. Ms. Barbara walked her path by working to meet the needs of children especially. For her lifelong commitment, she eventually becomes recognized as a national speaker and respected storyteller. Ms. Barbara shares with us how to identify our own talents as we walk the Red Road.

In the next to last selection of this section, we hear the voice of Mardella Sunshine Constanzo Richardson, a young woman who embraces her mixed heritage. She confronts the struggles and idealism of the young to change from a receiver to a giver, thus illustrating that the ideal of usefulness needs time to find its full expression through the special gifts of an individual.

Eastern Band of Cherokee poet Olivia Brown's poem closes this section. In "Native American," Olivia challenges non-Native stereotypes about Indigenous peoples. Hidden from racist view, contemporary American Indian peoples "make themselves useful" as highly educated "doctors, lawyers, and strong advocates for Mother Earth." In this way, they follow the footsteps of their highly accomplished and always active ancestors. American Indian communities are still here. American Indian women of proud nations are still here.

FURTHER READING

Anderson, Kim. *Life Stages and Native Women: Memory, Teaching and Story Medicine*. Winnipeg: University of Manitoba Press, 2011.

Anderson, Kim. *A Recognition of Being: Reconstructing Native Womanhood*. Toronto: Sumach Press, 2000.

Betasamosake-Simpson, Leanne. *As We Have Always Done: Indigenous Freedom through Radical Resistance*. Minneapolis: University of Minnesota Press, 2017.

Locklear, Tanya Holy Elk, and Margie Labadie. *Women of the Red Earth: A Literary-Visual Exhibition and Book*. University of North Carolina Pembroke Research and Creativity Showcase, 2017.

Wall, Steve. *Wisdom's Daughters: Conversations with Women Elders of Native America*. New York: HarperCollins, 1993.

Wilson, Alex. "How We Find Ourselves: Identity Development and Two Spirit People." *Harvard Educational Review* 66, no. 2: 303–18. https://doi.org/10.17763/haer.66.2.n551658577h927h4.

My Questions for Creator

Sometimes I wonder what Creator thought
When he created the nervous Native Child
Who was so unsure of the world he gifted.
I think on his intent in giving me the endless mind
The one that kept me up at night
The endless loop of fear and joy and fear again.

I wonder what he thought
When he made me look less like the rest
The words "You don't look Native" being my definition.

I ponder his purpose
In instilling the healer's heart
And making it feel so large it could hold the universe.

I request explanation
In asking me to live in two worlds
In the midst of my tribe and in the eyes of society and those
    who made it.

I ask his wisdom
In placing me here.
I want to help, but I am not sure if I can walk both paths.

Though I may never have these answers,
My voice can no longer be quieted,
Willed to life by curiosity and that endless mind.
Being called to sing my ancestors' song, even though I am not
    their mirror
Healer's heart beating rapidly
Helping to span the gap between the two walks.

The nervous Native child asked by Creator to speak with her
    people.
Hear the voice he has given me.

You Can Help Others Do More Than You Did

STARTING OUT ON THE FARM

As I share and reflect about my life, I could be as romantic as a poet like Robert Burns. I could romanticize some parts but not others. It was hard growing up. I, like most of the Indian people my age, started out on the farm, but I loved school. My mom was the one who pushed education, and she taught me to sing, so I loved that from the beginning, too. She and my dad went to the eleventh grade in high school. Then they dropped out and married. Not long after I started school, I knew I wanted to be a teacher. I always wanted to get an education.

Because of segregation, we did not have many opportunities. Back then, we thought our choices were limited to working on the farm, clerking in a store in Pembroke, or being a teacher. I knew I had to go to college. My parents and the community that supported education told us that this was our way to make a better life for ourselves. I never really thought about leaving home, though. I just wanted to teach because I loved doing things. I wanted to carry some of what I had learned back into the classroom. I knew I never wanted to work on the farm as an adult.

By the time I was about twenty, twenty-five years old, the tenant farms were becoming obsolete because of the mechanization of farming. There is not even a way for a small farmer to make a living today.

In the summers, we worked especially hard on the farm, working alongside family and friends. I remember that even when I was a senior in high school, I had to stay out and help pick cotton. Until the cotton was gathered, we would only go to school when it rained. To Dad, the crop had to be gathered. He did not look at the value of education the way Mom did. Mom was the one who made sure we could participate in the programs at school. Oftentimes, she would not be able to take us, but we could walk to school, and somebody would bring us home. One year, we were in a minstrel play, and we needed black hose. My mother did not have any nor a way to get to town to buy any, so she took some charcoal from the wood heater and made me some. She did things that other parents with ten children would not have done. She had all these children and grandchildren that graduated from high school and college. She was right there at every graduation.

"RUTH, YOU CAN DO IT."

I loved teaching, but a year after I graduated from college, Lonnie and I got married. He had graduated from Wake Forest the same year I graduated from Pembroke. After he taught for a year, he went to the army for two years. When he got out, he did not want to teach school anymore, but he could not get a job doing anything else in Lumberton. At the time, teaching was the only professional thing he could do. As an Indian man, he could not sell insurance, clerk in a store, or even get a job bagging groceries. So, he went to Charlotte because a friend of his from college told him he could get a job there as an insurance adjuster. When he got there, the firm would not hire him because him being an Indian, they thought that he could not represent the company to whites. Lonnie decided to stay in Charlotte, however, since he had sisters who lived there. We moved. I got a job typing for an accountant. I loved it. After tax season, one of the women in the office taught me some simple bookkeeping. When school started in the fall, I interviewed for a teaching job in the Charlotte City Schools. I was so scared because I had never really been out of Robeson County except for a short time. I remember sitting there when the administrator was looking at my application. He was not saying anything. I sat there thinking that if I had my application back, I would put "white" on it. I just knew that I would not be hired as an Indian. That was just the way it was—but I did get the job after all. It was the first experience in my life that made me say, "Ruth, you can do it." I have often wondered how my life would have turned out if I had not gotten that teaching job. In all, I taught for two years in Pembroke, one year in Charlotte, and fifteen years in Greensboro.

I remember one bad experience at school that taught me never to stop learning. I mispronounced a word I did not know while reading the paper in the teachers' lounge. Another English teacher embarrassed the daylights out of me right there and then because of that. I realize now that she did me a favor. I said to myself then that from now on, I would not open my mouth unless I knew what I was talking about. I observed my students when they pronounced a word that I had mispronounced. Instead of correcting them, I would write down the word and that night look it up. I told myself, "Ruth, you better listen, and you've got a lot to learn," and I did. I was far behind, but I never let it intimidate me. I asked to teach the drama course that no one else wanted. I made it into something that even the best students wanted to take. There were no Indian children where I taught, but I developed a course in American Indian literature. I did not get to do everything, but my students did. You do not have to do it all, but you can help others do more than you did.

WORKING TOGETHER: A LARGER PICTURE

Then one day at lunch, a teacher stated that Blacks were innately inferior to whites. I got out of my seat and stood up. I could not believe what I was hearing. It was shortly thereafter that the Guilford Native American Association came into being. I left teaching to become the first executive director. I loved teaching and the students, but I saw an opportunity to do more. Through teaching drama and literature, both American Indian and Black literature, I was gradually becoming more aware of the broader aspects of inequity. I recognized a larger picture. I started looking back at my own life, growing up in a segregated community and lacking opportunities.

I joined the Human Relations Commission for the city and learned even more. In 1972, I also began to serve on the North Carolina Mental Health Commission. Each month we met in a different mental health facility. I began to hear about and see children and adults who had been put away from their family because of lack of understanding, shame, or embarrassment. My interest in social concerns grew. In September of 1975, the local American Indian community started to organize. I was not involved at first. At community meetings, people spoke about what they needed. I became an advocate for people when the adults began to say, "I want to learn to read" and "I wish we could go out to a restaurant and sit down and read the menu."

At the Guilford Native American Association, I could do more than at school. We did not have much money to work with, but you had the opportunity to secure funding. It was an interesting time. Because of my role as executive director, Lonnie had to resign from the board and a woman became board chair. We were a first for the state: a woman executive director and a woman board chair. We set a precedent. I remember that the men in the other Indian organizations thought we would never make it—two women. On top of that, we had both been teachers, not businesspeople. They pointed out to us that we did not have any experience. I said, "If you are a good teacher, you have experience. All I had as a teacher was a roll book and some textbooks. I had to come up with the money and all other things I needed to teach drama." Others, however, helped us.

People can open doors for you, but if you do not have some to come through those doors who can do the work, nothing will get done. The organization and the development of the North Carolina Indian Commission grew stronger. Most of us were new at this type of work, but we learned together. We got help with capacity-building from the federal and the North Carolina state government. The North Carolina Commission of Indian Affairs was also instrumental in helping us. They could offer us a capacity-building grant that brought executive directors from the various Indian groups in the state together to learn not only about how to run organizations successfully, but also about learning to work together effectively. At that time, the different American Indian tribal groups had not much interaction with each other. We had not done much together, but at least we learned how to work for our own organizations. Many of us at the Guilford Native American Association were Lumbee, but we were not there to represent the Lumbee from Robeson County. We were all different, and the different groups learned to work together.

The Guilford Native American Association is a great success. We started out with educating people. Later we moved into social and economic development. We started Guilford Native Industries. We got contracts from industries and did piecework. We employed up to forty people, mostly women. These were the hard-core unemployed. They were women who had never worked, who were on welfare, who did not have enough education to go out and get a job. We hired them. Since they could not read, we had a code that only they would know on their time cards. This way, they did not have to feel embarrassed by their lack of literacy. They could pull their card and clock in and out. Some of them did well enough that we could serve as a reference so they could get a job somewhere else. We created a daycare center out of the money we made from the work. When people started to work for us, we could give them free daycare for two to four weeks to help them settle in. We worked with the city to help provide transportation. Guilford Native Industries was so successful that we presented our initiative in Washington a couple of times. The last major thing we did was help start a church, the Native American United Methodist Church. The Methodists were much more conciliatory, mixing Indian spirituality with Methodist traditions, than the Baptists or some of the other denominations. For example, their Indian congregations would have communion outside. They would use Indian fry bread, and when they were finished, they would place the remains of bread and wine on the ground to return them to Mother Earth. Simple things. We started out doing some of those things. We still have the drum. The congregation would sing and there would be an Indian flute playing.

We did work for Indians and non-Indians. One of the reasons we decided to offer the powwow and art gallery was to prove to the non-Indian community that we were Indians and that there are Indians in Guilford County. Many people were saying, "Oh, there are no Indians in Guilford County," because they were looking for the stereotype.

After teaching for seventeen years and working at the Guilford Native American Association for another twenty-two years, I was ready to slow down. I had burnout from the day-to-day responsibilities. They did not allow me to be creative anymore or to do some of the other things I liked. I retired from Guilford Native, but I was not ready to leave work. Today, I continue to serve on a volunteer basis for the powwow committee and help with fundraising and with the gallery.

A Firm Foundation to Withstand the Storms of Life

MAKE YOURSELF USEFUL, CHILD

You have asked that I share with you the highlights of the "Mary Ann Story."[1] I am always a little uncomfortable with this kind of request. I do not feel that I have done anything special, except to hang in there when the going was rough. To hang in there, one must have a firm foundation to withstand the storms of life. An individual develops a strong foundation through a conditioning of the mind that includes faith in God, belief in oneself, and reading inspirational materials. In my Bible, I have highlighted every reference to wisdom, knowledge, and discernment. I read a few of these verses to start the day. It does not matter what your beliefs are, the truths stated so succinctly in these words carry across all faiths. To be successful in life and business, you must have wisdom, knowledge, and discernment. I read these whenever I need to know that I too can overcome the obstacles on this road called life.

1. Mary Ann Elliott is addressing Cherry Maynor Beasley, one of the coeditors of this volume, in the opening sentence.

Hard work comes naturally to anyone raised on a farm of any kind, but especially a farm that not only grows the family's food for the year, but also is the primary source of revenue. Ours was a tobacco farm in Lumberton, North Carolina. This area is home to the Lumbee and Tuscarora Indians. Our farm was in an area settled by the Lumbee. My first memories are of working in the tobacco fields when I was three years old. Our family did not have a tractor. We had an old mule. It was the job of the very young children to ride on the sled behind the mule and hand a dipper of water to each of the field hands as you passed by. Children were expected to be productive members of the family. Whenever I got under my grandmother's feet, she said, "Make yourself useful, Child." To this day, I have a hard time just sitting around being idle. My "success" is the result of the hard work that began on that farm. That work ethic is still with me today.

Shortly after I started in the then very poor North Carolina schools, my mother moved the family from Lumberton, North Carolina, to the booming war town of Newport News, Virginia. The shipyard was hiring any able-bodied worker they could get to move into the area. Several housing developments sprang up to support the workers. Most of the workers had never lived far from their family farms in the South. Certainly, they were blue-collar workers with little to no education, but they were hardworking folks and had pride in what they did. I did not see myself as poor or deprived; after all, I now had a house with running water and a toilet—something that no one I knew back in North Carolina had inside their house.

WHAT YOU BELIEVE ABOUT YOURSELF
IS WHAT COUNTS

The first life lesson I want to leave with you is, what you believe about yourself is what counts. My mother's mother had died when my mother was seven years old. She was raised by a series of relatives. My mother struggled to obtain a nursing degree in the 1930s. She worked hard to save the $300 to attend nursing school, but the depression hit, and the banks closed. Having lost all her money, my mother went to stay with a relative and worked on their dairy farm in Laurinburg, North Carolina. She helped take care of the families' babies for two years until she once again had the $300 to attend nursing school. She did accomplish her dream of becoming a registered nurse under a three-year nursing degree program. She never gave up. She was an example for me to follow.

After we moved to Newport, Rhode Island, my mother went to work at the local hospital. My father went to work for a plant that supported the shipyard. He later started his own small roadside market. Today, you would call it a vegetable stand. Back then, it sold everything: meat, hardware, and even household items. My father also provided credit to the families of the shipyard workers. It was called Pud's Market. Pud was my father's nickname due to his love of hog pudding, something that I doubt most of you have ever seen or tasted. I was only in the second grade when I started to work at Pud's after school. I used an old hand-crank adding machine to total the groceries. I stood on three wooden Coca-Cola crates to reach the cash register keys. From my father I learned entrepreneurship.

It was not until I entered middle school that I realized that we really were poor, and that we lived on the wrong side of the tracks. The kids from the East Side made fun of the dress and speech of those of us from the other side of town. However, I made up my mind that I would be smarter and study harder than any of them, and that I would show them a thing or two. Lesson learned: if you really want to get ahead, you must apply yourself to the task.

YOU MUST ACCEPT CHANGE AND ADJUST TO NEW CIRCUMSTANCES IN LIFE

My later childhood years only spurred me onward to always try harder to be the best, to be first, in anything and everything. Then, when I was eleven, my father had a severe stroke. He had to stay in the hospital and a nursing home for a long time. My mother worked the graveyard shift at the hospital and then stayed through the early morning to take care of my father. I was sent to live with family friends. Lesson learned: you must accept change and adjust to new circumstances in life. It does little good to resist change.

This new family was wonderful to me. It was the first time since we had left North Carolina that the family sat down together, said grace, ate dinner, and talked to one another. They also lived in a single-family house and not an apartment, quite a change from the low-income housing where I had been living. Almost a year later, it was time to return home. I was needed to help care for my father while Mother worked. She worked nights and slept as much as she could during the day while I was at school. I took care of my father's needs after Mother left for work. Many of the nights were long and hard. I grew up in a hurry.

As too often happens, I started running with a group of older kids and began dating before I was thirteen. Then I met a handsome young man, and we were married just after my fourteenth birthday. I was sure I had met my knight in shining armor and that we would live happily ever after. I was pregnant. In those days, you could not continue school as a student or a teacher while pregnant. I dropped out midterm of the ninth grade. My three children were born when I was fourteen, eighteen, and twenty-two. The good news: my children and I grew up together, and they have all done very well. Marriage had its good and bad times, but we survived until my husband's death in a car accident in 1975. Suddenly, I was left with no education and no real job experience. What I did have was an aptitude for sales and a willingness to learn. I had been selling World Book Encyclopedias door to door. A dear friend helped me see that I needed to correct my very poor grammar and improve the way I dressed and acted. More than anyone, she set me on the pathway to success in the business world. Selling World Book taught me that you could fail many times and yet be successful overall. It taught me the real value of perseverance. It is a little like climbing a mountain. You may get tired, you may step in a hole or have to take a detour, but you must keep your balance and keep on trucking to reach the top. Never give up.

FIRST WOMAN WORKING IN THE FIELD

After World Book, I tried selling real estate, looking for more money to pay the bills and keep a roof over our heads. Then I heard that Motorola was hiring women for the very first time to sell car phones, a new phenomenon. At that time, they cost $3,500. Now, I thought, this sounds interesting, and any man who can afford one of these has to be rich and perhaps eligible. I must admit that finding a rich husband was my primary motivation at the time. I applied and interviewed in Norfolk, Virginia, but was told during the interview, "We have never had a woman working in this field before, and I am not sure you would be able to handle calling on our current and potential customers such as the construction and waterfront industries." I won that battle but lost the war. I did not get the job. Lesson learned: when you are out in the world of work and competition, is your goal the battle or the war? Lesson learned: pick your battles wisely. There are issues that are not worth fighting until the time and circumstances are right.

Motorola had an aggressive hiring campaign to employ women. They had been training their management staff. The Women's Movement was in its infancy then, but its impact was palpable. Eventually, I did get a job with Motorola. The first thing I was tasked with was to study a stack of very dry technical manuals. At the time, I did not know that on a two-way radio, you must push to talk and release to listen. It was only through the kindness of the owner of the local Motorola radio shop that I survived the training stage. Lesson learned: learn everything in your capacity about your area of work. Knowledge gains respect. After three years at Motorola and being number one in sales in the region without a promotion, I chose to leave. It was obvious that no matter what I did, I was never really going to get ahead there. Lesson learned: move on when the time and circumstances are not right for you.

I took a position with a fast-growing company in the infant industry of navigation and communication by satellites for ships at sea. I did not know what a satellite was, even less the mechanics of navigation. Still, I set out to read, study, walk the assembly lines, and ask questions to learn more. At the time, the major satellite firms were consolidating, and they very much had a glass ceiling where women were concerned. In 1991, following five mergers in eight years, I started Arrowhead, my own company, in the basement of my home. For the first two years, I did not pay myself a salary. I ploughed all revenue back into the business. From my first year's revenues of $60,000 to $100 million and two hundred employees in 2007 was quite an adventure with a lot of detours and a few false starts. I named the company Arrowhead to acknowledge my American Indian heritage and to get me to the head of any database. The original name was Arrowhead Space and Telecommunications.

Little did I know just how hard it would be to close a government contract or to receive the SBA 8(a) designation. This makes the company eligible for sole-source contracts up to three million dollars. Even after getting this designation, I did not understand how hard it would be to identify a potential project, wait for funding, and then finally get it under contract. This process sometimes takes years. All the while, you must stay in business and have enough revenues to pay employees and yourself. I can truly say if I had known how hard it would be, I am not sure I would have embarked on this journey.

MY SEVEN-DAY RECIPE

There were many starts and stops, but I learned to overcome obstacles, disappointments, and often just plain injustices. One experience was especially hard. I worked tirelessly with different governmental agencies to get large-dollar volume contracts for small businesses to encourage their growth and development. Large companies fought the change. Once the new policy was in place, we worked around the clock to respond to a major "Request for Proposals." Our proposal was rejected. All we knew was that we had been eliminated from the competition due to being technically noncompliant. After our hard work, after all of our efforts, after following the procurement for nine years, I was devastated. I went into quite a depression. Let me give you my seven-day recipe for overcoming this kind of depression and shock. First, spend two days in shock and denial. Your brain needs to adjust. Then spend one day crying, fussing, and raging at the injustice of it all. For one day, let yourself eat anything you want. My choice was Häagen-Dazs Decadent Chocolate . . . the entire pint. For one more day, go shopping for something you always wanted. Then get over it, get on your knees, say your prayers, be thankful for all that you have, and commit yourself to doing even better. It was only then that I set about trying to reverse the situation. The firm asked for a pre-award debrief, something that is almost never done. Our request was granted. It provided the opportunity to challenge the government findings. Many long hours were spent developing our strategy and response at the scheduled hearing. We made a commitment to be open and soft-spoken rather than confrontational and full of aggressive questions. Today, I am thankful to be able to share that we eventually won that contract. It was and still is the largest small business set-aside award ever made by the government: three billion dollars over ten years. In 2007, we had revenues of over seventy million dollars from this one contract. What did Arrowhead do for an encore following that award? They continued to progress by delivering innovative solutions that were in high demand. The firm also built the Cyber Warning Information Network, which provided the ability for many agencies to collaborate and share threat information following 9/11/2001.

OTHER DREAMS

As for me, I sold the business and retired. I then turned my life's direction to focus on other dreams and helping others to achieve theirs. Now I do quite a bit of charity work and motivational writing and talks. I find time to enjoy important things in life such as my family (children, grandchildren, and great-grandchildren) and friends (both old and new). I have used my funds to help others get a start in life, to support important work at UNC-Pembroke, and to honor those who helped me along the way, including my mother.

Learn your lessons on this road of life and leave a path for others to follow. Remember, today's mighty oak tree is just yesterday's nut that held its ground. Never give up.

Mary Alice, Play for Us

MUSIC HAS BEEN A PART OF ME ALL MY LIFE

I love music. Music has been a part of me all my life. It is part of all of our Indian people. We like to sing and play music. Of course, at my age, I cannot do it anymore. I first started playing music when I was about three or four years old, or at least before I started to school. I started by just picking out songs I heard. I learned to play on a pump organ I still have at my house. My papa would hold me in his lap and pump the pedal so I could. He would hum a tune, and I would play. After a short while, he wanted me to learn to play by reading music. He went to a friend and asked him to teach me how to read music and play. Papa also wanted me to keep up playing by ear. Papa's friend agreed, and that is how I now know how to play by ear and by reading music. I will forever be grateful to Papa for that. After several years, I started playing at family gatherings, at church, and at school. People would just say, "Mary Alice, play for us."

At that time, lots of us here sang by shape notes. We did not have instruments. Many churches did not have pianos, much less an organ. Often, to get the right pitch, the choir would start with a tuning fork. Someone would tune the group by singing, "Do, Re, Mi, Fa, So, La, Ti, Do." Someone else would start and follow by singing the tune of the song using shapes, "Do, Do, Ra, Ra," etc. The choir would sing the whole song just using the shapes. A caller would call out the lines of the song. That is how many churches and lay groups would sing a song. If I was there playing, they might start by asking me to give them a "Do."

I was just a teenage girl when the Baptist Men's Choir needed an accompanist. The regular accompanist was pregnant at the time and could not be away from home as much as they needed her to travel, so they asked me. There I was with those four or five men. We would get in one or two of their old cars, and here we would go off singing. There was always a singing somewhere about every weekend. We would practice at least once a week, usually every Thursday night. We would practice and sing, sometimes on Saturday and Sunday, just depending on what was going on in the community. We did not get paid, but those older men always made sure I had a way to go. Mama also made sure I had something to wear. I accompanied the choir until I was up in college. We had a good time. There was not much free time with all that focus on music, going to school, and helping around the house and farm. But I enjoyed it.

I went to school out here at Pembroke State College, now called the University of North Carolina at Pembroke. I majored in music. I was part of different music groups, and we would go to many places singing and performing. In college, we learned to perform all types of music, so that when I moved away from home, I had a good musical background. All the music students worked hard, so that whenever we went somewhere, we were well prepared. I remember that at first, some of the white students were surprised that the Indian students were so musical.

BECAUSE OF OUR COLOR

My dad's friend, who was Lumbee, and a white female instructor would take us wherever they could and let us perform. I can remember that we sometimes would go places, and the people there did not realize that there would be Indians in the group. Sometimes, the people would cancel when they found out that there would be Indians and Blacks in the group. Most people, however, did not care that we were a mixed racial group, but there were times that we as Indians could not go inside many of the nice places because of our color. I knew it was not right.

Singing and going to so many different places taught me about working hard and doing a good job. I also knew that I did a good job whether it was playing the piano, singing, or working on the farm. If you know within yourself that you are doing a good job, and you are nice to people, they often will turn around. If they do not, just move on. They will be the ones losing out. When I was teaching, I tried to get my students to see things that way. You just need to help people learn to do something well and then give them the opportunity to practice and do it.

When I finished college, I taught around here for about a year. I wanted to teach music and there just were not that many jobs. At that time, we had Indian schools. Most of our schools did not have music teachers. It was hard if not impossible for an Indian teacher to get a job in a white or Black school, especially in music. If a school had a position for a music teacher, it was usually only a position for one person. I eventually got a job teaching music in a school in Richmond, Virginia. I taught there for quite a while. At that time, teachers even in Richmond did not make much money, so I took a part-time job working at a church as the music director and playing the piano. I started out at a small church. Later, one of the teachers I worked with had a position as the director of music in a big church in downtown Richmond. He had to leave the job at the church, told me about it, and recommended me to the church. When I went in for the interview, they had me play for them. They gave me a piece of music and asked if I could play something like that. They were surprised that I could. We had played hard pieces like that in college. They decided to give me the position temporarily, as a trial at first. It was near Christmas, so they needed someone to work with the choir on the Christmas cantata music and performance. There I was teaching music at school, working at my first church, and helping this large church to get ready for Christmas.

WE BOTH LOVED MUSIC AND WE BOTH LOVED FAMILY

It was at that big church that I met my husband, Ed. When I first started the job, we were both dating someone else. We kept running into each other and having to practice together. A few months later he asked me out for coffee. Music allowed me to meet my husband. We both loved music, we both loved family, and we both were willing to work hard.

After we got married and were ready to start a family, I wanted to be closer to home. He had some family, too, but he knew I just wanted to be in Robeson County. We applied to Robeson County to teach but could not get a job. One year, one of us would get a job. The next year, the other. We just kept working on it. While we were trying to get a job here, we applied to graduate school to come back to North Carolina. We both started master's degrees at Appalachian State and moved to a town in the mountains. All the while, we kept trying to come back to Robeson. We finally got jobs here. I remember when they called me about the job, they said, "We have a job we can offer you, but you probably won't want it. It is at Knuckles, a Black school in a very poor section of Lumberton." I told them I would take it. Those children needed a good teacher just like everyone else. I had grown up poor, went to a poor school, and had taught in a poor school in Richmond. It did not matter to me, but they were surprised that I would accept the offer.

When we moved home to Robeson County, we did not want to live in Lumberton. We had moved back home to be close to Papa, Mama, and Grandma. So, we moved to Pembroke, and I drove to Lumberton to work. I went to Knuckles and made some great friends with my peers and their family members. We would put on plays and concerts. Those are important when teaching music and teaching people music is important, too. Several of those children later majored in music, but I was teaching them more than music. I was teaching them about self-respect, hard work, and about good ways of living. I have friends to this day that I made with that first job. When I served on some of the local boards, like at the hospital or library, I served with many of them. I think what the superintendent at Knuckles thought of as a negative became a strong positive for me. I could live close to my family and be in Pembroke every day, but I also got to know people in all parts of the county.

MUSIC GOT ME OUT IN THE ENTIRE COMMUNITY

All throughout that time of my life, I also played music at church every Sunday and on Wednesday nights for practice. Music got me out into the entire community. I would play at funerals for family, friends, and sometimes for people I did not know. I taught private lessons. I played for the Baptist Men's Choir sometimes. I was part of a television program about shape note music at UNCP. I have collected all types of music. I restored organs and pianos. I am not sure what is going to happen with all these instruments.

All these activities have helped to make me who I am. I became the first nonwhite principal at Tanglewood Elementary School, because people knew my work and me. I remember people saying something about me going back to school to take the principal's course. I accepted the position because I wanted to help change education. I was doing it one class at a time, which allowed me to think about every part of the school. I have a great life. I have not stopped to think about how music reflects who I am. I know many songs and read a lot of literature about music, but I just tried to fully live the life I have been given. I guess you could say music has helped shape my life.

Connecting Memory to a New Reality

AN INTERVIEW WITH CHEROKEE ELDER
MARIE JUNALUSKA

I have called the Qualla Boundary, better known as Cherokee, North Carolina, home for my entire life. Born and raised here, I only left this land to attend college and graduate school. As an enrolled citizen of the Eastern Band of Cherokee Indians, my identity is rooted in this seat of our sovereign government. Yet, most importantly, my identity is grounded by the people of this place and these mountains that cradle us here. I was raised to listen to the stories of those who came before, and I have been honored to share those stories both as a high school teacher and as a writer. These stories are where I have always found the essence of who the Cherokee are because they carry the values of our people and the wisdom of our natural world. It is my hope that my two sons and my students come to know these stories, these storytellers, as guideposts for their own lives as well.

"I wasn't sure you meant *this* coffee shop. I realized we have more than one now." Marie laughs as we tuck ourselves into a booth in the back corner of Qualla Java. Though the two of us make up half the clientele, the shop is loud with the sputter of brewing coffee and rubber soles against a sweating concrete floor. "I know. I thought the same thing."

Much has changed in Cherokee, North Carolina, since the last time Marie Junaluska and I spoke, and this is an unusual place for us to meet. I have known Marie, a fluent Cherokee speaker, educator, tribal leader, and translator, my entire life. We never meet at coffee shops. We see each other at ball games, school functions, and tribal government events. She is the mother of one of my childhood friends, and she worked for my aunt Hazel beginning when Marie was fifteen years old. Unless it is a business meeting, locals rarely meet friends in coffee shops to chat. Of course, things do change. "What used to be here?" I ask her as we settle in. Marie was born in 1950, so I am eager to get a glimpse into the world my parents' generation knew. "Like when you were growing up. What did it look like?"

"There has always been a bridge here. Yes. Always a bridge."

As she continues to piece together her memory of the place, we realize that what was once a part of her childhood life is now underground, blacktopped over—a concealed Cherokee we never think about. Tunnels, perhaps—like the ones on shows like *Unearthed*. We enjoy the mystery of it, but I cannot help but lament knowing I will never see it and wondering if we can ever access it again.

This is Marie's role, though. As a translator, she makes visible the invisible. She connects memory to a new reality. She is motivated by her own desire to see and know more. Marie has been speaking Cherokee her entire life. Her mother spoke nothing but

Cherokee to her and her siblings. That is not to say that she has been a student of the language in the way we prepare our current generation to be. She grew up immersed in oral Cherokee. Written Cherokee, the syllabic system developed by Sequoyah by the 1820s, was not accessible to her as a child. I assume I know the reason. Other than the Bible, books in area homes were not typical when Marie was growing up, regardless of whether it was a Cherokee home or not. I, as is often the case, am wrong about that reason, though. Marie clarifies, "When the Cherokee capital was moved from New Echota to Red Clay, the printing press was destroyed by the Georgia Guard. Everything was destroyed. I think material stopped being printed at that time. I think the material available at that time was put on a shelf. . . . Those that knew how to speak it taught us. Then as far as the schools here, we were not teaching it at all until the 1970s."

I have heard most of my life that the Cherokee language was nearly eradicated because of boarding schools. I often forget the impact of other federal assimilation policies and practices. An act so simple as the destruction of a printing press over a hundred years ago still influences language education today. The language only survives because of people like Marie and her family. Language was, and largely still is, carried in the minds and mouths of Cherokee people and rarely in the books and papers of dusty archives. A language must live to survive. People like Marie give it the heartbeat to do so.

Marie's mother only taught her two characters of the syllabary—the characters for Jesus: tsi sa. Those two characters continue to fascinate her, as if there is a key to a secret door; the language, fully realized, is that key.

While attending day school in Wolftown, North Carolina, Marie was taught by her only Cherokee teacher, Oscar Welch, in the fifth grade. For the remainder of her formal education, Marie does not recall having another Cherokee instructor. It is not a fact that seems odd to her. "I never really thought of it," she tells me. As the only Cherokee faculty member on staff at my local high school, it is something that troubles me, though. I am concerned more by how few Cherokee language teachers we have in our community who have both the skills of language proficiency and teaching methods. These are rare individuals.

Like many of her peers, Marie left home after eighth grade and attended Riverside Boarding School in Oklahoma. Stories of boarding schools in Indian Country range from transformative to tragic. For Marie, Riverside emboldened her commitment to language and culture. Ironically, being farther from home gave her perspective to appreciate the uniqueness of Cherokee culture and her gift of language. When she could speak with other Cherokees, she instantly returned home. Sharing her distinctive gift, she discovered an allusive appreciation from strangers. I watch her smile as she recounts her days at Riverside. Her memories call her attention back, and her face seems to grow more youthful in the retelling. She knows I understand what it is like to go away to discover home.

At Riverside, she also recognized her role in a larger Native community. "It made me so proud that I could speak our language and I could hear the others speak their language. I thought, wow, we have our own too, and so we would proudly speak it," she recalls. "It's what really opened me up to our culture, our customs. Taking me away from here and seeing. Today,

I am so thankful. It was a very meaningful . . . just a rewarding experience for me to go away from here . . . and get to know all these other Natives from different states. . . . Otherwise, I would have kept thinking we were the only Indians out here."

When Marie returned to North Carolina, she knew she wanted to be a teacher. Marie's Oklahoma experience exposed her to new possibilities to put both her knowledge and her approach to teaching to use. Cherokee Central Schools received a grant to teach the language, and Marie applied to work with the program, primarily because it gave her the opportunity to both teach the language and learn the Cherokee syllabary in the process. "It was typical that most people did not have experience with the syllabary. I think it's been dormant," she recalls. Through this teaching opportunity, she could pursue the key she had only glimpsed as a child in those two syllabary characters her mother taught her. "I had no idea how to read and write," she remembers. "But I was ready. I was excited."

As I sit across from Marie, I already know the timeline of her career. Marie was a Cherokee Tribal Council member for most of my life, so I try to imagine her as a young teacher. It is hard for me to visualize how one makes the jump into a political life. Cherokee politics are notoriously contentious. Marie is soft-spoken. I have never heard her raise her voice. I am quite sure I have never seen her frown. She is reflective and kind as she talks. Mind you, not in that stereotypical "wise sage" way that is likely expected by the tourists who sip lattes in the next booth over. We joke about her encounters with other tribes while in Oklahoma and politics in Cherokee, but she is never mean-spirited. Her gentle demeanor comes from a place of wisdom and insight, not indifference or witlessness.

"I was pregnant when your grandmother, serving on council at the time, came to me and asked if I would work as the interpreter for tribal council. It kind of floored me. It was kind of scary. But I thought maybe I could do it because I could speak." Two months after giving birth to her first child, Marie began her career as an official interpreter for the Eastern Band of Cherokee Indians. She worked with mentors such as Beloved Woman Maggie Wachacha, whom she calls "jolly," and quickly learned the art of translating English legal documents into the Cherokee syllabary. Her work sustains and strengthens Cherokee sovereignty. As legal professionals do, Marie interprets law and its intent—and that is just the first step. She is the bridge between our desire to self-govern and nation-build, and its implementation.

"Why did you decide to run for council?" I am always fascinated by this question. Marie is a council member who served prior to and after the gaming industry came to the Eastern Band. Therefore, she has seen incredible transitions and, perhaps, motivations of our people. "It was the peoples' thought. Not mine. I never even thought about running or being a council member. One day I was in Painttown for a Community Club meeting, and I thought, well here I am. I am living here and have kids. I should be down there and see what's going on. I just started attending sessions, and the next thing I know, they asked me if I would consider running for council. And I thought, *Oh, no! No!*" We laugh together. "I immediately said no, and that person asked me again. And I said maybe the next term. But the next term didn't happen. They went ahead and put my name down."

And this is where my age shows. Marie is telling me that she never signed up to run for office. She did not choose to run. She did not name herself a leader. She smiles at my surprise.

She knows that I am used to modern Cherokee politics, where so many candidates are self-ascribed leaders, not put forward in the traditional way of a community call to action. "So, I went ahead. When I look back, it makes me feel good that the community did this. So, I have looked up to the community since," she explains.

When days got tough, and they often do in tribal council, Marie refocused herself at the source—she returned to the old homeplace to talk with her mother. She returned to peace and simplicity and a single, Native language. "Whenever we were having council and we would cover so much . . . at the end of the day . . . I would go home. I mean home where I was raised. I found that it was calming. It was like coming back down to earth. It was like slowing down. We would speak Cherokee and talk about what went on. It was a calming time—get my senses back. Language is more peaceful in the Cherokee language than it is in English." Until her passing, Marie's mother and her old homeplace served as a conduit to the peace of the language. She still goes back to the old homeplace, and of course, she plays with her eight grandchildren when her world needs more peace.

As a writer and English teacher, it goes without saying that I am fascinated with words. While I am nowhere near fluent, I enjoy learning from our Cherokee speakers and especially discussing difficult words to translate. Translation, after all, is about worldview, and quite often English and Cherokee worldviews collide. So, I was curious to ask Marie if there were any words that she had difficulty translating from Cherokee to English—that she felt like just never really rendered fully. She thought for a while. As a woman who adeptly translates legal terminology, Marie is rarely tripped up by new words and effectively uses the resources of the Language Consortium (comprised of speakers from all three Cherokee nations) to decode any tricky terms. "To-hi" (pronounced *tow he*), she finally answers. "Yes, probably that word." The basic translation of this word is peace, but of course, it is more than that. It is a lifestyle perspective of peace—a complete peace that requires mind, body, and spirit to be aligned. It is why Marie calls the language "peaceful." It is why so many Cherokee-speaking mothers swear that correcting a child in the Cherokee language is far more effective than the same command given in English. It is a peaceful approach that is not weak or passive. *To-hi* is an active, all-inclusive peace.

I almost hesitate to ask Marie the question I know she and other Cherokee speakers always get: "What is the future of the language?" Within that question is imbedded a connotation that it is endangered, some would even say dying. Anthropologists, linguists, and documentarians have trickled in and out of these mountains for decades fascinated by the possibility of standing in the moment, in the place, of an actual extinction. Sometimes it is as if they want to be among the last to witness it. Sometimes they want to posit a plea for rescue. Never have there been any easy answers to insuring the survival of the Cherokee language.

Marie is ready for it. She is adamant and sits up in the booth, resting her coffee on the table. "Will we save the language? Absolutely! I will not say it is dying. I resent that statement. It is not a true statement. The [Kituwah Language] Academy has done so much. It's already beginning to live. I feel confident that it is going to live on." When I ask her if she has any other language goals to accomplish in this lifetime, she speaks of her days of coming into the language. "I want the children to be able to read the Bible. That will be the ultimate," she relays. Marie's goal stems both from a spiritual standpoint and the recognition that the Holy Bible is the most comprehensive collection of translated Cherokee vocabulary available. I think this confuses outsiders sometimes—the reliance of Christianity for Cherokee cultural perseverance. However, the text is intended to convey peace, capturing the connotation of the language more accurately than any other translated work of literature.

I joke, "To be able to write Jesus in the syllabary, right?" She laughs but expresses her wish that she could spend more time teaching her grandchildren the way her mother taught her.

"So, after traveling and enjoying your time learning from others so much, what is it about this place? I mean, of course, outside this coffee shop. Why return and stay here?" I ask.

"What is it about this place? Well, this is the land. Where our ancestors were. Where I was born. This is home. We are totally blessed to live in a place like this. There is no other place like it," she speaks as if the answer is obvious, which I personally think it is.

After our meeting, Marie sent me an email. She had forgotten to mention a project very important to her, one that I was familiar with: the Right Path Leadership program. The Right Path, *Du-yu dv-i*, "program provides unique leadership learning that tailors contemporary leadership development competencies from the wisdom of Cherokee ancestral cultural leadership."[1]

1. http://cherokeepreservation.org/what-we-do/cultural-preservation/lifelong-leadership-development/the-right-path/. Accessed November 11, 2021.

Essentially, the program translates Cherokee leadership values into modern practice. Marie's translation talents are not simply related to words and phrases. Translating Cherokee and English is about moving forward in the Cherokee way. It is sovereignty and cultural vitality. It is the essence of a thriving culture—change without sacrificing core values and worldview.

Marie reminds us, "When the language goes, our culture will go with it because it is all entwined." I am leaving the coffee shop with a sense of peace, though. Marie is responsible for this *to-hi*. She embodies it, and her life's work takes an active responsibility for ensuring that our history, culture, and worldview translates into the future. There has always been a bridge here, and if Marie Junaluska has anything to say about it, there always will be.

To Be a Part of It

MY PERCEPTION OF LIFE

What I am sharing here is my perception of life. I can only speak of that which I know or of that which I perceive. I am considered a storyteller. I never gave myself this title. Traditionally, being a storyteller means to be the wisest person around and to know many things. My grandmother was a wonderful storyteller and so was my dad. When people started to introduce me as the storyteller, over time, that is how I got the title of storyteller. I am honored to carry that title. The storyteller is one of the most respected and revered persons in any Indian community. I did not reach this point of my life easily.

I grew up in Robeson County in eastern North Carolina. I was the oldest daughter in a family of nine siblings. My dad was a sharecropper and sometimes a tenant farmer. My mother had to help work on the farm to make a living for us. As the oldest, I was responsible for taking care of my younger siblings, guiding and teaching them. I remember always admiring the natural world around us. There is not much of my childhood that I can remember, but what I do remember is my love of art and my desire to be a teacher. My favorite pastime was to look up at the sky. I marveled at the beauty and the wonder of the clouds. I re-member thinking how great it would be if someone could paint a picture that beautiful.

We all live in something called the circle of life. As we go through this circle of life, we find different roads. Each road leads us to a destination. At each of these destinations, we find things that we can accept or things that we can reject. I am on the last part of my journey in my circle of life. In my teaching and my art, I am in a place that I feel good about. I have learned that my most important life lessons were the ones that I had to wait for. Education provides knowledge for us, but there is a part of us deeper than knowledge. In that place, our spirituality comes into play, also the part that we must be in our golden years. It is the part in us where we have made progress over time. In each phase of our life, we learn different lessons. Each of those lessons prepare us for the next lesson to come. If we skip one lesson or if we skip one phase and move on to another, we will not be true to ourselves. We will not be happy. When we are young, well, maybe I should say when I was young, I was very impatient. I wanted what I wanted right away. I wanted the finest things, especially American Indian art. I started collect-ing American Indian art. I have learned now that those things are not so important. They are not important at all, not to me. I hope that they will be important to the people to whom I will give them.

The one thing that has been a part of me as far back in my life as I can remember is my special connection to the natural world around us. I feel the need to be a part of it. I feel a need to play in dirt, to dig in the dirt, to take a walk in the woods. This is where our real education comes from if we will only take the time to listen and to be in tune with the natural world around us. If we only take the time to pay attention. To go into the woods. To just listen to the sounds around us. To listen to what our inner voice is saying.

BEING SIDETRACKED ON THE JOURNEY

The biggest mistakes on my journey are the ones that I make when I fail to listen to my inner voice. Some may call it intuition. When my inner voice is speaking to me, when the spirit is leading me, I am learning to pay closer attention. I am learning that this is the voice taking me to my destination. I need this voice to lead me as I continue my journey through life.

I am not a prejudiced person. I take knowledge from wherever it comes. Then I will take the knowledge that I have, and I will apply it to my own life. I will use it where I can. I will depend on the spirit to teach me how to use that knowledge. It might be one of my biggest prayers right now that I will pay closer attention to my inner self, to the spirit that guides me, and to the natural world around me. I think that for us to be true to ourselves, we must do that.

Sometimes, I was sidetracked along my journey. There is a story that I tell about someone coming from outer space. He ran into space debris, and his spaceship was knocked off course. He needed to look for help to get back on course. That is what I have had to do from time to time. My prayer is also that I will live a path that is a good path, a path that my children, my grandchildren, my great-grandchildren, and all the generations to come will be able to follow and maybe glean something from it. I now see that what is truly important is not the things that I leave behind, but the path that I make for others to follow. If I can make a path or if I can say something or do something that will be of help to one person along the way, then I feel like this is a good thing, because sometimes it is hard to find a path that you want to take or a path that you feel is worth taking.

THINGS WILL FALL IN PLACE

I have touched many people's lives by the things that I do. I am more than a wife, a mother, an organizer, a teacher, and a teaching artist. I am a community person. I am a peaceful person who loves being able to do things for others. If there is a need, I seek a way to help meet that need in someone, especially in children. American Indian children today are suffering for so many things. They are suffering for material things, but mostly they are suffering for guidance. They need guidance. They need someone to give them a helping hand and to encourage them. I remember from my own childhood what it is like to have low self-esteem, to not have the things that you need for school, and to feel that your clothing is far below what the other students wear. My heart goes out to children who do not have the things that they need. I live in Charlotte. Thousands of children here are homeless. Some of these children are Indian children. I try to find sources and resources for food that I can take to the families to help them feed their children, especially in the summer months when they are not going to school to get break-fast and lunch. For some children, those are the only meals that they get.

For many years, we have also put together a Christmas cele-bration for the American Indian children in the area. I could not do any of this without the help of other people. I believe that our Creator sends people to help. Strangers will come with bags of candy, with bags of fruit, and tell me, "I am here to help." We named our children's Christmas celebration the Dennis Lowry Memorial Christmas Celebration after one of the Indian people from our community. Mr. Lowry and his family have been so generous that now we are able to provide Christmas boxes of food and fruit baskets for our elders as well. It was as if someone said to me, this is your mission, this is what you are supposed to do. Just when I think that there is no way I can do this, a way is being made. If there is a need and our Creator keeps making a way, it is possible for me to help meet those needs. If he is guid-ing me in that direction, then that is what I will do.

I am not saying all these things to talk about what I do. When it comes right down to it, I really do not do anything. I am a vessel by which things are getting done. I am not financially or physically able to do them on my own, yet the need is always met. Last year, I told a young lady who has been very helpful to us over time, "I don't think I can do this anymore. I am just not able; it's just too much work." She said, "You don't have to do it. We just need you to organize it. We will do the work, but we need you to be the one that brings the children in. You just find the children, and we will make sure that all the work is done." After that, she brought her friends to help. Also, last year, one of my Indian neighborhood kids who is now an adult went out and bought a pickup load of toys for the children's Christmas party. The spirit works in this way also. If there is a need and if you are on the path that is intended for you to take, things will happen. Things will fall in place. They will be what they need to be. If I can do the things that I do, with the help of all these wonderful people and with the Creator allowing me to do it and make a way, then I will continue to do these things.

When my time has run out and it is time for me to stop, someone else will be there who can pick up and continue. I believe that if there is a need for it, our Creator will make a way for it to happen. I say to anyone who is wondering about how to live their life or how to reach their life's goals, be true to yourself. There have been times in my life where I was not true to myself. Those were the times when I made mistakes and had to seek guidance to get back on my road. If we are true to ourselves and if we listen to our inner voice, we can reach our goals. There is nothing wrong with having ambitions and goals. The sky is the limit to anyone who wants to reach out and grab it. If that is your goal, your heart's desire, and your life's passion, then it will happen if you work toward it, if you are true to yourself and if you follow the direction that the Creator is giving you. I believe that it is our inner self, our inner voice speaking to us.

I hope that I will listen more to my inner voice because there are still so many lessons that I need to learn. One of the most important things I have learned is that the more I learn, the more I realize how much I do not know. There are so many things that I want to experience in the time I am still here. I hope to be able to reach out and to touch others. Most of all, I want to be able to really be in touch with my inner self and with the spirit that teaches and leads and guides me. If I do that, I believe that I will reach the end of the good Red Road. I think it is the road on which we all need to be. It is the road which will lead us to our final destination.

Our People Are Moving in a Positive Direction

CHILDHOOD MEMORIES

I am the maternal grandchild of Mardella Sunshine Lowery of the Lumbee Tribe of North Carolina. I am the paternal grandchild of Carmella Mazzitelli of Lametiza, Italy. I was born and raised in Philadelphia, Pennsylvania, where I attended a Catholic school from first through twelfth grade. I was named after my maternal grandmother whom we call Mommom. As a child, I always knew that my family was different from my friends', but I did not really understand the full weight of those differences. I am a member of the Lumbee Tribe of North Carolina and a first-generation Italian American. My Native and Italian cultures were infused into my daily life in ways I did not realize or understand until later in life.

My childhood memories are filled with dancing at powwows and educational showcases, dancing with my Mommom along with my sister and cousins. I also have vivid memories of the smell of my grandmother's house and the big family meals with all my aunts, uncles, and cousins that we enjoyed there. I have fond memories of visiting family in Robeson County and in

Greensboro for weeks at a time during the summer. At the start of my senior year of high school, I secretly applied to the University of North Carolina at Pembroke without telling anyone in my family. I had not taken a formal tour of the campus, but I felt drawn to it. I also felt drawn to the American Indian Studies program. I was so elated when I received my acceptance packet in the mail. When I applied to UNC-Pembroke, I had this fairytale idea of how beautiful it would be to go to a school surrounded by Native students, especially people from my own tribe.

PROVING MYSELF

When I moved to Pembroke to attend UNC-Pembroke in 2005, I experienced a lot of culture shock. First, my people were not exactly the most welcoming. I had to prove myself as a non–Robeson County born Lumbee and as a mixed-heritage Lumbee. I did not attend the local Purnell Swett, South Robeson, Fairmont, or Lumberton high schools. I did not know anybody of my own age. I dressed funny to some people. I constantly had to ask people to repeat themselves because accents threw me off. I had no clue what the Harley Rally or what cruising were. I was Catholic, not Baptist or Methodist. Secondly, my Mommom spent so much time pouring into me what it meant to be Indigenous and what it meant to be Lumbee that I was shocked that so many young people did not know simple things about Lumbee history and culture. I just assumed they would have learned those things by growing up in the tribal territory, but that was not the case. My Mommom explained to me that growing up in Philly, I had to know everything to defend myself, explain myself, and educate others. My siblings, cousins, and I were always the one percent in our schools. If you grow up surrounded by people who are exactly like you, you do not have to constantly fight those little battles. You live and breathe your culture daily without realizing it is "unique" or a part of your large tribal culture. For centuries, Lumbee people have been battling the world around them because of our race and culture. If you go back to Jim Crow days, Lumbee had no place in the white world of segregation. UNC-Pembroke was founded as a teacher training school so that Native kids could have a school to go to as well as help at home when they needed to.

When I arrived, many people thought that it was not important to teach Lumbee culture because it was being lived. During the decade that I *lived* in Pembroke, I saw a cultural shift and awakening happen. I saw the youth wanting to learn more. They took it upon themselves to do so. I saw it becoming commonplace to talk about Indian culture and to talk about the Bible all in the same conversation. However, there are over fifty thousand Lumbee—and in this large community, Lumbee children are raised differently, and therefore, young people experience life differently. I saw young Lumbee leaders step up and work with Lumbee educators to work on bridging the gap. It was a slow process, and some people were, and remain, resistant to these changes. Their choice does not make them wrong. However, our people are moving in a positive direction. We are not only educating ourselves about our own history and culture, but also about other tribes, especially those within our state.

I eventually found my way and cultivated lifelong relationships. While I was a student at UNC-Pembroke, I had the opportunity to learn how to bead. I also had the opportunity to make my first regalia as an adult, meaning I was over the age of eighteen years old at the time. I engrossed myself in dancing and singing at powwows, which were already a familiar space for me. I was always confused and unsure how to respond when other Lumbee students would make comments as though they were not really "Indian" if they did not powwow. The same people who judged me for not being Lumbee enough now stood before me not seeing their own issues with Indian identity. I do not see powwows as a defining factor in my "Indianness," but it helps soothe those homesick feelings.

I was also able to learn how to weave pine needle baskets from Ms. Loretta Oxendine. I learned the history and importance of quilt making. I learned why the church has played such a pivotal role in our communities. I learned the deep farming roots and history of Lumbee people. I began to understand how my peers were living and breathing a culture, which they just saw as ordinary everyday life.

OVERCOMING THE IMPACT OF COLONIZATION

Self-identity plays a dynamic role in our self-esteem. When we are teenagers and young adults, we start to establish who we are and lay the foundation for the adult we will grow into being. To spend those years considering yourself less than the Indian stereotype that society says you should be, could be detrimental on multiple levels. Lumbee people do not fit into the Native imagery created by Hollywood. Through the centuries, Lumbee people have had to fight to be who they are, and continuously prove who they are.

Geography made us a part of Indigenous peoples who had early and prolonged contact with the colonizers. This is not our fault. To this day, the federal government and other tribes work to break us down, degrade our name, discredit our Indigenous identity, and belittle our youth. Sadly, those tribes who aim to pull us down do not realize how they have adopted and implemented the colonizing mindset that arrived in this land centuries ago. There are countless documented stories of how first the British and then the U.S. governments have pitted our people against each other in the hope that we would exterminate each other.

The landscape in Indian Country has changed a lot over the years, largely in part due to the internet and social media. Lumbee creatives are now able to network with other Native artists. They have forged dynamic bonds that would not have been possible in the past. We have also seen our youth transition from young adolescent leaders in high school to young adult leaders in their communities. The women and men who were able to participate in the North Carolina Native American Youth Organization and the National United Indian Youth boards and conferences have also been able to build relationships with emerging leaders from other tribes. Today, well-connected young people make sure that our own people learn and keep alive the Lumbee nation's story.

Native American

Native American:
What do you see?
Teepees? Buffalo? Primitive living?
What do I see?
Doctors, lawyers, and strong advocates for Mother Earth.
We are still here,
Hidden by our education and modernisms.
Do you see us?

. . . .

Contemplating Words of Wisdom by Our Women Elders

Listen to the elders.

Create space for children, especially children that you did not give birth to.

Create sacred space at work. Work is a sacred activity.

Tell your stories and share them with the youth. Dance and sing with them.

Whenever we were to be separated from our parents, Dad would say, "Remember, we are only a prayer away."

Anything worth doing is worth doing right.

Do not ever forget your past. Carry it with you daily.

PART TWO

Spirit Medicine

Introduction

Throughout this volume, American Indian prayer and ceremonial life constitutes an active and integral part of the woven tapestry of women's voices and experiences. This section gathers poetry and stories that move prayer, ceremony, and movement of spirit onto center stage. Since time immemorial, matrilineal and matrifocal extended family structures sustained Southeastern Indigenous societies and determined economic, political, and juridical life. Oral traditions and ceremonies transmitted the meaning and ethics of these ancient woman-centered systems by commemorating and honoring female creator beings such as Selu, the Corn Mother. Woman-centered political and social institutions such as that of Iroquoian clan mothers have structured Indigenous lifeways for centuries. As this section tells us, the clan mothers resurface in unexpected ways when needed most. Sacred female beings such as the Three Sisters and Selu, the Corn Mother, manifest their meaning and presence when needed most.

Despite centuries of colonial assault on traditional lifeways, women still know, practice, and experience the arts of Indigenous prayer, skillfully shifting their heart awareness so it can perceive deeper structures of reality. Women carry this knowledge forward as they cultivate a good mind: spirit medicine works through and as spirit, works through and as thought. It is medicine because a good mind creates positive outcomes.

In her poem "Some Indian Women," MariJo Moore evokes the strength of a good mind, which always also exists on a continuum with other-than-human manifestations of being: thunder, sun, and lightning. The poem names another foundation of traditional Indigenous prayer and ceremony, that of continuous world renewal, the world's immense capacity for replenishment and survival. In her essay "Spirit Medicine," Kim Pevia models for us how to trust the world's innate power of renewal, or as she describes it, "It's okay to say that we want more." A certified life coach, Kim also points to finding our way back to a good mind that is cultivated in Indigenous prayer: to see the world with the eyes of the heart.

Daphine L. Strickland's story maps intergenerational trauma and, specifically, its transmission from mother to daughter throughout the span of five life-changing years that end with the death of her mother and Daphine's change of status as she becomes the new matriarch of the family. Driven to exhaustion and despair by trying to care for a foster child with fetal alcohol syndrome, Daphine learns to acknowledge the truth of her own childhood abuse. As her mother is becoming increasingly consumed by illness, Daphine discovers an inner strength and power as an Indigenous woman. She names this newly found strength the Clan Mother within her. As in a blood memory, ancient Southeastern patterns of female leadership emerge when needed most. They guide and assist.

Author Christine Hewlin illustrates how Southeastern Native women's traditions of prayer and ceremony can continue in a Christian communal framework. Her story encompasses almost forty years of her life. Its narrative arc follows the spiritual pattern of world renewal that began with her adult baptism. For some nineteenth-century missionaries to the Cherokee, the Christian ceremony of baptism by immersion was reminiscent of the ancient ceremony of "going to water." Since the Southeast has been historically a "water rich" cultural resource for all Southeastern Indigenous communities, it is very likely that different versions of river ceremonies were practiced for millennia before the arrival of Christian missionaries. Baptism by immersion in revered rivers such as the Lumber still take place today. Sometime after her baptism by immersion, Christine's life turns around when she begins to trust the work of the Holy Spirit.

The final two contributions in this section add the dimension of land as sacred home for Native women. Nora Dial-Stanley's poem "Not Anymore" measures the damages that colonialism has brought upon Native nations, especially the loss of homeland, the loss of "a sense of truly belonging. A place to call her own/ Where her children would always live, learn, and teach our Native Ways." In the poet's view, the loss of homeland brought about the loss of women's strengths and rights. Colonialism undermines women's right to be safe and free, to be "a true woman warrior of her tribe [as] before the invasion." Grieving the immensity of the loss, some traditions that have existed since time immemorial, however, remain even if in weakened form. These include "the Beat of the Native Drum," storytelling, planting and honoring the Three Sisters, and canoeing and swimming in the culturally powerful three rivers that carry the same names as the Native nations they nurture, the Lumbee, Coharie, and Waccamaw.

Charlene Hunt's story also works with the theme of sacred land. The author documents an Indigenous woman's spirit of reverence in evoking the Three Sisters in her family garden. And as is true for Daphine Strickland, in a moment of greatest need in caring for a loved relative, an ancient female presence makes herself known and brings comfort and knowledge: the Corn Mother, one of the Three Sisters.

FURTHER READING

Allen, Paula Gunn. *The Sacred Hoop: Recovering the Feminine in American Indian Traditions.* Boston: Beacon Press, 1986.

Anderson, Kim. *Life Stages and Native Women: Memory, Teachings, and Story Medicine.* Winnipeg: University of Manitoba Press, 2011.

Awiakta, Marilou. *Selu: Seeking the Corn-Mother's Wisdom.* Golden, CO: Fulcrum Publishing, 1993.

Dorris, Michael. *The Broken Cord.* New York: HarperPerennial, 1990.

Duncan, Barbara Reimensnyder. "Going to Water: A Cherokee Ritual in Its Contemporary Context." *Journal of the Appalachian Studies Association* 5 (1993): 94–99.

Emanuel, Ryan E. "Climate Change in the Lumbee River Watershed and Potential Impacts on the Lumbee Tribe of North Carolina." *Journal of Contemporary Water Research & Education* 163, no. 1 (2018): 79–93.

Lowery, Malinda Maynor. "Lumbee Indian Women: Historical Change and Cultural Adaptation." In *American Indian Women of Proud Nations: Essays on History, Language, and Education*, edited by Cherry Maynor Beasley, Mary Ann Jacobs, and Ulrike Wiethaus, 9–23. New York: Peter Lang, 2016.

Mankiller, Wilma, ed. *Every Day Is a Good Day: Reflections by Contemporary Indigenous Women.* Golden, CO: Fulcrum, 2011.

Mann, Barbara Alice. *Iroquoian Women: The Gantowisas.* New York: Peter Lang, 2000.

MariJo Moore

Some Indian Women

Some Indian women carry the sun in their eyes,
Thunder in their throats and lightning in their hands.
They can see through the darkness that sometimes rains,
Speak above strong ill winds, and touch the hearts
Of hurting children, smoothing out fear and neglect.

These women are important to all the people.
Not only because they are gifted
But because they know what it means
To share deeply, face the adversities of advancement,
Pull back, replenish themselves, then share deeply again.

Some Indian women carry the sun in their eyes,
Thunder in their throats, and lightning in their hands.
They are the multifaceted, marvelous, mysterious
nature of our survival.
We must honor them.

Spirit Medicine

If I had to create an image for myself, I think I am a bridge between two worlds. Between two kinds of thought processes, sometimes between the two parts of a paradox. The light comes through at the broken places.

I moved to Red Springs because my brother and sister-in-law live less than a mile away, and they have kids. My dad lives down on Queen Road. I am still an insider outsider here. The first year was challenging because I could not find any work. I would drive around, fascinated by places that would make my spirit heavy. I kept having a sense that great bloodshed or great pain or great trauma took place there. I could feel it. That was when I knew that to be here was a paradox: to love this land and at the same time to take care of myself in this space. I prayed and I smudged. I had to come back for a part of me that exists only here. This is a new dance. I am coming to understand fully that it is the dance of family, tribe, and life. We have everything we need here.

I am a life coach certified by the Coach Training Alliance. I like to say, "Here is the information" and "let's practice it in a place that's safe so you can actually take it and use it in the world." So much more is within our power than we realize. Awareness of that changes how we walk and how we talk. I am an open and friendly person by nature. I move through the world aware that I am Native American. It does not have to separate me from anyone. I greet people as if I have a heart with an eye in the middle. I practice looking at people with the eyes of my heart so I am not seeing anything that would keep me separate from them. We are all carrying something. We do not touch each other lightly enough. Even when we walk up to a stranger, if we look away, it is different than if we look at them and smile. There is no such thing as neutrality when it comes to this human dynamic.

WE HEAL DIFFERENTLY

To work in our world with our own people, we need to know that we heal differently than the majority world. One of my first questions to my clients is, "What's your spiritual practice?" That question is not about how many times a day we pray. It is about what we do to tend to our spirit. Our spiritual practice can be *I walk, I fish, I play ball*. We can cultivate it as a place of refuge. When we are quiet and turn to the earth, we get whispered to sometimes. There are words. That is what has always been and will always be. Wake up! Wake up!

Fear is insidious. From a psychological point of view, about 90 percent of our decisions are fear-based. We are not even aware of where those fears are. If we begin to get still a little bit more, if we have a little bit more self-awareness, we can understand where those fears are that are stopping us. My personal struggle is in delivering my message about change. When we are in pain, historically traumatized, and already feel powerless, change just feels like another wound. The message is, "It is okay to say we want more." The message is that it is okay that we want more for our children and for our community. I consider myself a bridge to where we want to be or where we could be. I want to help raise the next generation of leaders. We also need our elder folks' talent, their energy, their expertise, their experience, and their time to make change.

I am a visionary. I am connecting with my Creator in a "show me" way. I know I tell crazy stories, but I can only tell my stories the way I experienced them. Here is a "show me" story. One day while still living in Florida, I was driving to the beach. I always parked in the same place, maybe within a few parking spaces, in the same general location. I put my blanket down in the same place. The regular people I would talk to always were there. I had been praying for a partner or some other shift. I wanted something to change. As I was driving to the beach that day, I could not find my spot! I knew inside my spirit that something was going to be different that day. I kept driving up the beach, and I ended up four miles north of where I normally park. I found a new spot. I put my blanket down, and I knew and could feel energetically that something was going to happen. I am thinking that I am going to meet my guy! I am like, "Yeah, my man's around the corner." I am thinking it is going to be something amazing. So, I am sitting there, the beach is packed, I mean packed—and I started crying!

An overwhelming sense of loneliness came over me that I have never felt before. I felt like I could go drown myself in the ocean; it was that deep. I knew the feelings were not mine. It was just a deep sense of loneliness. It was like a collective sense of loneliness. I began to have this thought that this loneliness was not about me. It was a question-and-answer session of some spiritual place that was not mine, but I was sitting here with all these people around me. I wondered who would be open to a conversation.

THE HEART AND THE EYE

I looked at different individuals and thought, how would I know whom to engage? From the wounded places that I felt, I knew I could not talk to anybody because if they had rejected me, that would have just put me in a deeper despair. It would add to the loneliness. In all great visions, inventions, or evolutions, there is a question and there is an answer. The question came to me: how would I know if a person was open to a conversation? In my mind's eye, I saw the heart with the eye, like a logo. I was there with that loneliness and when I saw the heart with the eye, the loneliness passed from me. I knew I had returned to my normal state of being. I got home, and I drew the heart and the eye. I called it "The Connection Project." I wrote a business plan. People could wear the heart and eye as jewelry; see the symbol on cups, hats, and t-shirts. All it says is that "I'm aware"; "I'll see you with the eyes of my heart"; "I'm aware that we are in this together"; "We are connected." I created a whole series of questions for people who do not know how to talk to strangers.

The symbol of the heart and the eye within it is our culture to the bone. One of my favorite Native American expressions is, "The medicine you need grows right outside your door." I believe that right next to us is the person who will introduce us to our love or our next business partner or the one that has the answer to the question with which we have been struggling. Right next to us.

Stories such as this one are coming back. As we tell the stories, we understand that we are not separate from each other. As we reconnect to our culture, to the sacred, and to the divine, they are the answers that will begin to come for us in a very real way.

I have learned to trust that whatever comes up is divine. I know that I am an odd duck. We all are. It is the beauty of being unique and original. As we come to fully embrace that truth, we understand that we do better shining as ourselves than trying to be somebody else. As we trust the divine, then things can change and shift because we are free to be ourselves.

Daphine L. Strickland

···

Clan Mother

INTRODUCTION

"Clan Mother" is the story of Yellowbird, a woman asked by her mother to accept a ten-year-old boy into her life. Yellowbird had promised to raise the boy in the event of her mother's death but then is requested to fulfill her promise sooner than she had planned. She does not know how to say no to her mother. Once the boy is living in her home, Yellowbird learns that they share some of the same hidden suffering. The boy's behaviors wake memories that she had tried to bury. She soon experiences what it feels like to have her home, her family, and her mind taken over by a child with an unacknowledged history and troubling symptoms. Yellowbird struggles to care for the boy, her family, and her own needs. She tries to stay sane while her world crumbles around her. At first, she fights to control her world as she had always lived it. Gradually, Yellowbird learns to adapt to change, something that we as humans try to control and shape but cannot.

The story of "Clan Mother" describes a journey from suffering to understanding the deeper self that lives within women. In the Iroquoian tradition, a Clan Mother has been responsible for advising the chief as well as the whole village. Her family has the power to choose and remove a chief. In the clan, she is a wise woman held in high esteem.

CARING FOR A DIFFERENTLY ABLED
AND TRAUMATIZED CHILD

It all began in the spring of 1987 when Yellowbird's mother asked her to consider keeping Tommy, Yellowbird's adopted brother, for the summer. After much thought and discussion with her husband, the couple decided that because of legal and insurance issues, they could not welcome the boy into their house on a part-time basis. Yellowbird told her mother that they would consider adoption instead. When they went home for Easter, Yellowbird's mother had the boy ready to return with them. It was at this moment that the Yellowbird I once knew began a struggle. She had to survive changes that were taking over her life. You see, Tommy had many problems at home and in school.

The school assured Yellowbird that trained teachers with years of experience could deal with any type of children. They promised her that Tommy would be fine in a regular class. Then Tommy's paperwork arrived at the school. On the evening of his first school day, the principal asked Yellowbird to his office. When she arrived, Tommy was hysterical. The principal was at a loss to explain what went wrong. Yellowbird took Tommy in her lap, crossed his arms in front of him, and put her arms around him. She held him close so that he could calm down. She would learn much more about restraining Tommy to bring him calmness in the days, months, and years ahead.

On that evening in the school office, Tommy yelled repeatedly, "He tore my notebook! He tore my notebook!" When Tommy calmed down, he said the principal had ripped his new note-book while carrying him to his office. The principal informed Yellowbird that a teacher had stopped Tommy for running down the hall to catch his bus. What neither principal nor teacher were aware of when stopping the child and carrying him to the school office against his will was Tommy's fear to miss the bus home and the fact that he did not like to be touched. Tommy's reasons for this dislike became clear much later.

Yellowbird told the school principal that she had no profes-sional training to help children like Tommy. Yet it was Yellow-bird, not the principal, who had calmed down the child. She also insisted that since the principal had assured her of the school's expertise in working with children like Tommy, he had failed that day.

She would learn more about Tommy's additional behavior is-sues at home and at school as time went on. These behaviors included attacking teachers and others (including Yellowbird), stealing, cursing, and lying. Yellowbird used all the resources she had at the time to survive. To Yellowbird, it was as though her home was being attacked and she could not stop or con-trol the invader. Tommy directed his aggression and abuse to-ward Yellowbird, her daughter, and anyone else he experienced as a threat. She had to check her groceries, her bedroom, and her daughter's bedroom regularly. Tommy took items such as money, food, or toys without asking—anything that he saw and wanted—and then hid them in his room.

There was one more issue. Tommy was only ten years old, yet he knew the language and sexual behaviors of a much older per-son. The child's open display of adult sexual knowledge lured Yellowbird back to her own childhood memories. She began to recall her father's so-called friends who abused her when she was a child. Until she lived with Tommy, Yellowbird had managed to bury these memories. Now they were bubbling back up to the surface of her mind. She was struggling not only to regain control of her own world, but she also had to contend with Tommy's world. She felt helpless and used by her mother, who knew of Tommy's condition yet had kept the information to herself.

In April 1989, two years after Tommy had moved into her house, Yellowbird injured her right hand. It required surgery. She lost partial use of the hand, and the company where she had worked for ten years now had no job for her. Yellowbird had always been a self-reliant "superwoman." She would do anything for anyone. She worked until a task was completed, no matter how long it would take. Losing her job left her feeling empty and void. Her unemployment seemed to have stripped her of her identity and self-worth. The fact that Yellowbird no longer had to work should have been a blessing, because taking care of Tommy's needs had turned into a full-time job. Work had been difficult sometimes. In the previous two years, however, work also had been her means of escape. Now the boy consumed all her time. Yellowbird resented Tommy for his control over her life and for having triggered the hideous intrusive memories that she thought she had long since put away.

THE CLAN MOTHER

Change was on the way. Yellowbird's mother underwent open-heart surgery and suffered a stroke. The mother that Yellowbird knew died with that stroke. There was a body, but the mother she had known and loved was gone. A different woman lay paralyzed with a tracheotomy, occupying her mother's body. Yellowbird's responsibilities now included caring for her mother as well.

Through taking care of her ill mother, Yellowbird drew another woman from within: a Clan Mother. Until her mother's illness, the Clan Mother was unknown to Yellowbird. The Clan Mother could take charge because Yellowbird listened to what was changing inside her. The Clan Mother cared for the shell of what once had been Yellowbird's mother.

A second change took place. Tommy had threatened to kill himself and was admitted to a mental hospital. Hospital staff evaluated his overall health. The insurance company appointed a nurse to keep the family up to date about medical decisions and new information about Tommy's health condition. Importantly, the nurse also was able to secure Tommy's case history documentation from the Department of Social Services. She told Yellowbird that neither her mother nor anybody else should have adopted Tommy. Instead, Tommy should have been placed in an institution. The doctor's recommendation was to move Tommy to an expensive group home in Georgia, but Yellowbird's family's insurance refused to cover the costs. When Tommy returned from the hospital after thirty days, Yellowbird finally had the information she needed. She knew that she had to act to save herself, her family, and her marriage. For his own safety and Yellowbird's family's protection, Tommy was moved to a group home.

With Clan Mother's guidance, Yellowbird could manage anything, and that is what she did. She had learned about Tommy's special needs and saw to it that they were cared for professionally. While Tommy lived in a group home, Yellowbird continued to take care of his finances. She had him tested further and found out that he suffered from fetal alcohol syndrome and several learning disabilities. She spent many hours writing letters and talking to people to get his educational and psychological needs met.

SISTER SELA

Yellowbird's sister, Sela, was her friend and supporter from the time she took Tommy into her home. Sela provided her with information about Tommy's alcoholic mother, his previous foster homes, and past troubles at school. She discovered that Tommy had suffered physical and sexual abuse in foster care long before their mother adopted him. It was Sela who Yellowbird talked to each day. They shared each other's burdens. It was Sela who diagnosed Yellowbird with an asthma attack the first time that Tommy went on a rampage at home. It was Sela who managed to get him out of the house and to Yellowbird's husband. The two sisters were soul mates and had become each other's lifelines.

In June 1991, Sela died after suffering twelve years with lupus. The illness attacked her heart and lungs. Yellowbird had refused to acknowledge the truth that Sela's heart could not keep going. Yellowbird had never allowed the thought of Sela's death to enter her mind, even though her sister had spent the last five months in and out of the hospital. Sela was young. After Sela's death, she felt she had to be strong for her sister's family. Of course, she could do that. She would be there to help them, but a part of Yellowbird died along with Sela.

TRANSFORMATION: THE WOMAN IN THE MIRROR

The Clan Mother who had started taking care of Yellowbird at a time of great need now takes care of everything. Yet Yellowbird does not recognize herself when she looks in the mirror. She sees someone else. She sees her mother. She does not want to see her mother in her own face because her mother had not been honest with her. Her mother had used her just as all those sorry men had used Yellowbird when she was a child. Her mother knew the depth of Tommy's problems, yet she had set in motion a path of destruction that almost annihilated Yellowbird and her family. No. Yellowbird does not want to see the image of her mother in the mirror.

Yellowbird promised her mother that she would take care of Tommy, and she does. Yellowbird's house does not look the same these days. There are papers everywhere. "A place for everything and everything in its place," is not the way she wants to live her life at this time. She will not answer the phone; she will not let it ring. The answering machine is always on. Yellowbird stopped answering the phone the day she got the call telling her of her mother's death in January 1992.

Look again. Who is the person in the mirror? It is Yellowbird, who looks like her mother but is herself transformed. The Clan Mother takes care of the appointments. The Clan Mother cooks the meals and attends the many meetings concerning Tommy in schools and in the courts, even though he lives in a special home for children with extreme behavior problems.

TAKING MY PLACE IN THE CIRCLE OF LIFE

In 1992, one year after the death of her sister and with Tommy living safely in a group home, Yellowbird finally began receiving counseling for the abuse she had suffered as a child. She was able to put together the old parts of Yellowbird that she wanted to keep, along with the old memories that were not overshadowed by revolting and painful ones. She discovered that Yellowbird was in real trouble that originated in her childhood. She also discovered that in the old Iroquoian tradition, the Clan Mother had come into her life to save her.

Today a new Yellowbird is emerging slowly, just as a butterfly comes forth from its cocoon. A Yellowbird who sets boundaries for herself. A Yellowbird who is learning to love herself and, most importantly, who is learning and laughing at herself and others. For the first time in her life, she is not taking life so seriously. She is playing and making new friends. She will live the rest of her life much better than she did during the first fifty-one years. Good-bye young, innocent Yellowbird. Hello, older, wiser, loving Yellowbird who is good to herself and to those with whom she shares her time. This Yellowbird loves the Yellowbird in the mirror. She is learning to stand up for herself. She is learning to be in harmony with herself and the world. This Yellowbird is super, but not superwoman. She has taken her place in the circle of life.

Today, I am proud to be the woman in the mirror, and I am proud to be my mother's daughter.

Bruises of a Battered Woman

Life deals us countless kinds of bruises. Many women are carrying around hurts that are not visible, caused by the abuse of a parent, a spouse, or other people with whom they have had relationships. Wherever the bruises come from, they bring with them physical, mental, and emotional pain.

OH MY GOD, WHAT HAVE I DONE?

Things were very difficult for my family when I was growing up. We were a family of six, and even though we did not have many material things, we had each other. My dad worked and did his best to provide for our family. However, early on, we lost my three-year-old baby brother to an illness that was unexplainable. No one shared with us what caused his death. It just seemed like my dad had lost hope and did not know how to cope with what had happened. After that, things seemed to get bad. I knew it was hard for my parents, so I would go to school and try to find ways to make money to help. The only way I would get new clothes was by working and buying them myself.

During that time, greeting cards were popular, so selling them became my source of income. Later, I sold flower and garden seeds. By the age of ten, I had begun to gamble to earn fast money. In my teenage years, my parents forbid me to go anywhere. I could not spend the night with friends. My dad would not let me have a boyfriend like the other girls. I realized later that he had my best interests at heart. He was only trying to protect me. If I only had known then what I know now.

At the age of thirteen—without my parent's permission—I began seeing a young man who was older than I was. I was naive enough to believe that he was the one with whom I would spend the rest of my life. Despite my romantic fantasy, it was nothing like I had imagined. The very act of losing my virginity to him was both painful and guilt ridden. Within a year, he had moved on to another young woman who was closer to his age. Consumed with anger, all I could think about was how he had used me. This was the beginning of a very painful time in my life, and the start of a long cycle of hurtful and disappointing relationships with men.

By the time I was fourteen, I had met another man. He was ten years older than I was. After only a few months with him, rebellion set in. I would get up each morning, get dressed, and let the school bus pass by. Instead of getting on the school bus, I would go over to my cousin's house, because I knew that my lover would either already be waiting for me or that he was on his way. Initially he was good to me, and we had fun together. I could not wait to look into those beautiful eyes. After a few months of being with him, I discovered that I was pregnant. I was so afraid. I lost my virginity at thirteen. Now I was in the ninth grade and about to become a mother. I had to confide in somebody.

I told my mother. She was very upset with me. We kept it a secret from my daddy for as long as we could. It was not long before he started to notice that my clothes were fitting me differently. He would tell me to pull my skirt down; which of course, I could not. The truth finally came out that I was pregnant with a twenty-five-year-old's baby. My dad confronted my baby's father, and they got into a violent altercation outside. After the baby's father tried to slit my dad's throat, my dad in turn tried to shoot him. Everyone inside the house, including myself, was scared. It all blew over after a short while. The two of them made peace for my sake and the baby's.

On May 31, 1975, I began to experience some pain, but I did not know that I was in labor at the time. My daddy, my mom, and my baby's father had all been drinking. Despite this, I rode to the hospital with them. Early the next morning I gave birth to a 5-pound-13-ounce baby boy. I was only fifteen. I did not have a clue about how to take care of a baby. Although she did not take over, my mom taught me the basics of how to feed and bathe my son. One day my boyfriend built up the nerve to ask my dad if he could marry me. Dad said no because I was too young. Nevertheless, things seemed to be going well until I discovered that I was pregnant again. I asked myself, "Oh my God, what have I done?"

How was I supposed to tell my parents that I was pregnant again? I could not. It became my secret for a while. Eventually, I told my mom. One night my dad got in some trouble, and before he was arrested, he asked my mom if I was pregnant again. And of course, the answer was yes. I was very sorry about my father's arrest, but I was relieved that I did not have to break the news of a second pregnancy to him face-to-face. I had not even gotten used to having one baby, and there I was seven months pregnant with a second and had not yet seen a doctor for prenatal care. Although I would not have gone through with it, fear and panic caused me briefly to consider the idea of abortion. On August 3, 1976, I became a mother for the second time. I was sixteen years old with two children, no help from their father, and receiving $103 monthly from welfare. Of the $103, I had to give $50 to my father. I knew I could not take care of us on fifty-three dollars a month. I hired a sitter so that I could work. It was hard for me to leave the children every day, but I had to do what was necessary.

My children's father worked at the same place as I did, but before he made it home, he would lose his earnings gambling. It was bad enough that he was not supporting his children, but he had the audacity to ask for my hard-earned money—the money I needed to pay the sitter—just so he could gamble. He had also begun drinking heavily. I became tired of seeing him drunk. I did not want our children to see him that way, either. After we finally broke up, I stayed home a lot, because there was not anything else I could do.

A NEW AND DIFFERENT WORLD

One day, my neighbors invited me to go to church with them. At first, I hesitated because I did not see any reason why I should go to church. Eventually, I accepted their offer and took my two children with me. I went to a few Sunday services and later attended a revival for a few nights. I accepted Jesus as my Lord and Savior. I remember sitting in the pew when they gave the altar call. I got up and went to the front. As the weeks went by, I did not do any of the things that I had normally done before. I stayed at home with my children. However, as time went on, I became bored. The life I thought I wanted was not exciting any longer.

On August 18, 1977, I turned eighteen years old. I could now show my ID and buy my first beer. I had finally become an adult, but I was not aware of the problems that came along with being an adult. One day, I was sitting at home. I heard a loud rumbling noise coming from around the corner. I looked out to see a pulpwood truck. Oh, my goodness, my heart skipped a beat when I saw who was driving! He was so good-looking! I found myself waiting every day to see him come by. I finally had my chance one Saturday night at a small neighborhood pool hall. After introducing ourselves, we sat and talked the night away. We left early in the morning as the sun was rising.

It was the Sunday I was supposed to receive baptism. At that point, I was not sure I wanted to go through with it. Back in the day, they did baptisms in a pond. When it was my turn, someone led me by the hand down to where the preacher was. I was nervous and afraid to go under the water, but they took good care of me. People were hugging me as I had never been hugged before. They welcomed me by extending to me the right hand of fellowship. After everything was over, I knew that I had entered an entirely new and different world. The church building did not have air conditioning, so they opened the doors to allow the breeze to come through. I had been out all night without any sleep, and I remember the refreshing feeling the breeze brought over me.

When I got back home, everyone was drinking and partying. I remember thinking, *How am I supposed to be different coming right back into the same environment?* I knew I had a new church family down the road, and a Bible, but I still was not strong enough to cope with what was going on around me. It was hard for me because I had no spiritual guidance at home. I did not know who or how to ask for help.

Shortly after my baptism, I found out that the people who had introduced me to the church had backslidden. I became confused. I stopped going to church. Not long after that, the young man I had stayed up all night with became a regular part of my life. He would visit me at the house, and we would have the best conversations. However, how many of you know that a person never tells all? The devil let me hear only what I wanted to hear.

A VOLATILE SPIRIT OF JEALOUSY

I finally met his family. They were nice people. They were financially stable, owned their own business, and lived in a pretty home. They shared many things with me, but I learned the hard way that their son was troubled. We had only been dating for a short time when I realized that he had a volatile spirit of jealousy.

One night, he went to the pool hall with some of his friends. He encountered some people who did not like him. After getting into an altercation with one of them, the man said he was sleeping with me. All hell broke loose. I tried calmly to discuss the situation with my boyfriend, but there was no reasoning with him. Then it happened. He hit me in my face and bruised my eye. I could not walk away then because I was afraid that he would follow through with the threats he was making. Hitting me, he also caused damage to my children, my brothers, and my parents. I was ashamed to be seen in public. He eventually apologized, stating that it would never happen again. I forgave him.

Things were good for a while, until one night he decided to go to the club. I was at my mom's house. It was getting late. Upset, I went to look for him, driving his car. However, once I got to the club, I was too afraid to enter. I knew he would not like that I had come to find him. I left and as I was driving back home, the car broke down. A man stopped and offered me a ride. I accepted. When my boyfriend got home, I met him outside, because I knew he was going to be angry about his car and the fact that I had gone out looking for him. As soon as I approached him and attempted to explain what had happened, he began to accuse me of being involved with the man who had given me the ride. Becoming enraged, he tore my dress off. He proceeded to beat me. I do not even remember how we got to his mom's house, but I do remember what my face and body looked like the next morning. When I looked in the mirror, I thought, *Oh God, this can't be me!*

My lips were so swollen they were turned inside out. My back was so bruised, it looked like a leopard's. I had a broken nose. He took me to the hospital. I lied about what had happened. I told the police that my car had broken down and the man who stopped to help me tried to rape me, and when I fought back, he started to beat me. The police clearly did not believe me, but they could do nothing. After I left the hospital, I had to face my children and the rest of my family. I was ashamed of how I looked and ashamed that I had lied to protect him. While I healed, I stayed at home. It was unbearable to go out in public. The abuse continued to occur more frequently. I was not sure how to escape the torment. All I knew was that I was a frightened young woman who had never experienced anything like this before. As the months went by, we would have a couple of good weeks, and then things would completely unravel. He would revert into becoming that same violent monster. The beatings would start all over again.

[*Christine was in and out of this relationship until the boyfriend was killed. She entered other relationships that were also abusive, but she eventually managed to escape them.*]

ALL THINGS ARE POSSIBLE IF YOU ONLY BELIEVE

I struggled to make ends meet because of my gambling habit. As I matured, I became weary of the life I was living. The club scene was not the same for me anymore. I looked at how the people were dancing and behaving, and it no longer made sense. I believe that God was drawing me back to Him. I would get home and my youngest daughter would ask, "What did you drink tonight?" I could truthfully respond, "Pepsi." When she turned seven years old, she asked me if she could be baptized, and I told her yes.

I was still gambling at the time. On December 3, 1999, I lost a lot of money. The next morning, my youngest daughter asked me for something, and I could not afford to buy it. I knew it was time to make a change. The day after Christmas, she was baptized, and I gave my life back to the Lord. I was not sure I could raise her without Him. This time, however, something was different. I decided to allow the Holy Spirit to work in me. My desire became to please God, not my flesh. I began to experience Him taking away my old desires and replacing them with something new. Where before there was bitterness and hatred, now there was forgiveness and love. I was able to put the past behind me and move forward with my life.

The more I read God's word, went to Bible study, and stayed in His presence, the more I was transformed. Through the washing of the Word of God, I was able to release the shame, pain, and hurt of my past. Sure, I still made mistakes, but I had something on the inside to warn me when I did. I could go to my heavenly Father to ask for forgiveness. I also had godly people around me to support and encourage me, rather than the worldly ones I was around before. My family had started to go to church as well. My dad and I entered a closer relationship. God delivered this bruised and battered woman out of almost three decades of a lifestyle of abuse, fornication, and gambling amongst other things. God has done some extraordinary things in my life, and I believe that He is going to do even more for me and through me, for His glory.

I finally went back to school. In November 2013, I earned my GED. Today, I sing in the choir. I am the president of my church's usher board. I have a beautiful family. God has shown me that it does not matter how we begin. It is how our life ends that really matters. He saved my soul. He delivered me out of a life I thought was impossible to escape, and for that I am truly grateful.

If He did it for me, then He can do it for you. With God, all things are possible if you only believe.

Not Anymore

Brown Eyes
       Brown Face
              Black Hair
This should be the norm and not the exception
In a land that her ancestors called home for thousands of years
But not anymore.

The Sounds of Native Songs
              The Beat of the Native Drum
                     The vision of Traditional Dancing
This should be the norm and not the exception
In a land that her ancestors walked, lived, loved, and died for
   thousands of years
But no more.

Storytelling
      Speaking of our Language
                  Hearing the sounds of the Woodpecker
Watching the Eagle and Hawk fly into Father Sky
                Watching the Turtle on Mother Earth
Not so much.

Planting Corn, Beans, and Squash
    The Three Sisters
        Hunting the Deer and Turkey without boundaries
        to feed and care for her family
Not so much anymore.

Canoeing
    Swimming
    along the Lumbee, the Coharie, and the Waccamaw Rivers
Not as often as before.

The right to be free
        The right to be safe
            The right just to be
A true Woman Warrior of her tribe before the invasion
Not anymore.

A sense of truly belonging
    A place to call her own
        Where her children would always live, learn,
        and teach our Native Ways
Not ever anymore.

Farming Always Brings Us Home

American Indians were the first farmers in what is now known as the American Southeast. The story of the Three Sisters is commonplace within all American Indian tribal communities. Corn, beans, and squash planted together to help each other grow. The concept of companion planting, in which one plant helps the other, is the basic idea behind the Three Sisters. Farming goes back generations in many American Indian families; it was our means of supporting our families and has a deep spiritual connection not only with the Earth but also with our souls. Farming always brings us home.

These roots run deep within my own Lumbee bloodline. My great-grandfather was a tobacco farmer. My grandfather and my daddy, Charles, whom I am named after, followed in their footsteps. As a child, I can remember that my feet loved being in the dirt, and even though I am an adult, I still get barefoot in my own garden. Thinking of the smell of tobacco as it hung curing in the "bacca" barn takes me right back to my childhood days. These memories provide good medicine for my mind, body, and spirit . . . not just for me, but for many of my tribal people. The lessons the fields taught us at an early age are carried and passed down through the generations just like the storytelling of the Three Sisters.

Last year while being down home, I was in the garden with Daddy. He had a look in his eyes that shook me to my core. "Daddy, are you okay? Daddy, do you know where you are?" He was lost in his own garden. He was lost in a place that has been part of his life for years, the place that has given him joy and pride as he bragged about how big his tomato plants were. I could tell by looking at his expression that he did not know where he was. He was confused and lost, and I could see this in his eyes. It was as if someone had briefly turned off his light. Slowly and with fear in his voice, he asked, "Where am I?" Hearing my Daddy ask that while we were standing in the middle of his own garden brought tears to my eyes and a sharp pain in my belly. Despite the unexpected raw emotion welling up in me, I knew to stay calm so that I did not alarm my father. I quickly grabbed his hand, looked him in his eyes, and said, "We are in your garden, Daddy."

In that moment, I was forever changed. My strong father, now seventy-six and hair full of white, was not only visibly aging, but also now it was painfully obvious that his mind had also started to fade. As the sun set while I was standing there in the garden holding my daddy's hand, I realized that my life was about to drastically change . . . and my mind drifted to the story of the Three Sisters. Standing there watching the sun's brilliance disappear made me think of his memories that were also starting to fade. . . . What if he forgets me?

Since then, our family roles have changed. I spend more time visiting my father and providing caregiving and support for my father—the man who helped make me who I am today. Now, I am the strong one—like the corn plant in the Three Sisters story—helping to hold my father up. I know that one day he will be too weak, in mind or body, to do this on his own.

Contemplating Words of Wisdom by Our Women Elders

Know and value yourself! You are wonderfully made. You are here for a purpose.

Seek the hawk within yourself.

Honor the ones that walked before you.

Decide where your home is.

Sacred space is sometimes as simple as listening to other women.

PART THREE

Getting Justice When There Was None

Mary Ann Jacobs

· ·

Introduction

Traditional Native American justice is rooted in notions of relationship and dialogue rather than adversarial dispute, harmony and balance rather than proof and guilt, and renewal rather than punishment.[1] Colonization and the resulting historical trauma still haunt our communities. The clash of Native and non-Native cultures continues. That clash is acutely visible in the American and Indigenous views of justice. The American justice system promotes values and practices such as individualism, self-actualization, and state-sponsored revenge and punishment, usually in the form of fines or incarceration. The system's focus is on the vilification of the offender.

In contrast, Indigenous restorative justice views both the offender and the victim as respected members of the community who have valued roles within the group. Part One of this volume describes in detail how these valued roles are taught from childhood onward. In Indigenous restorative justice, both the offender and the victim have equal value. The negative behavior of the offender is viewed separately from the perpetrator's core identity, which is not vilified or seen as evil. To resolve a

---

1. F. David Peat, quoted in Hand et al., p. 449.

violation of communal ethics, both parties and their extended families are brought together with a peacekeeper who works to seek a mutually agreeable outcome. As some scholars have noted, "Ideally, the goal of a peacekeeping intervention is for all parties to leave feeling that a satisfactory solution has been reached, and in compliance with the restorative practice, the family of the wrongdoer ensures that restitution is made (to the victim) and compliance followed."[2] In all cases, Indigenous restorative justice, as is true for American justice, expresses the cultural norms of the community. In Indigenous communities, restorative justice seeks a return to balance and community health by assisting the victim and by educating the offender with careful attention to their respective family networks.

The communities represented by the authors in this volume are mostly non–federally recognized tribes without fully functioning Indigenous judicial systems of their own. Their stories and poems reflect both the American and Indigenous worldviews of justice. One can see ideas about individualism, self-actualization, and revenge at work in the stories and poems as well as the values of relationship, community, and the equal worth of all people to the community independent of their behavior. Often, the authors are taking the long view of justice, because the stories and poems are a part of their lived experiences. There is always hope for a future that will bring greater understanding of the past and the human beings who will at some point be elders themselves.

2. Hand et al., 2012, p. 453.

Gayle Simmons Cushing's poem remembers Native women from generations before her own and those beyond. She describes Native women of all ages with all the roles that they may inhabit, including caring for children, cooking, teaching, farming, and professional careers. Amongst all the doing, there is still plenty of room for the mystery of creation.

Ruth Dial Woods gifted this book with a portion from her dissertation, which describes her journey to the Indians of All Tribes (IOAT) occupation of Alcatraz Island in 1969. The occupation lasted from November 20, 1969, to June 11, 1971. Dr. Woods visited Alcatraz Island to represent the Lumbee Tribe. The Lumbee Tribe's administration at that time was the Lumbee Regional Development Association (LRDA). The IOAT leadership of the occupation had issued a call for tribal representatives to come to Alcatraz to attend the "American Indian Conference of All Tribes." Her story is a very personal recalling of the history of the Alcatraz Occupation written from the perspective of a Lumbee woman who had never lived on a reservation or experienced a Bureau of Indian Affairs (BIA) boarding school. Although the IOAT's occupation of Alcatraz Island lasted nineteen months and did not result in all the demands the occupiers sought being realized, Alcatraz marked the beginning of American Indians waking up to the power of body-protest to seek justice.

My and my daughter's essays about the Black Lives Matter (BLM) protest by University of North Carolina at Pembroke (UNCP) students in June 2020 are paired together to offer the reader two views on the same protest march. My daughter and I supported and do support the aims of the UNCP students' march. We went for different reasons, however, and viewed it from the perspective of our different lived experiences. The viewpoints of people who do not support BLM or the right to protest the actions of the police are not represented in these two stories. While it is possible to misread the aims of the BLM group and their slogan "Black Lives Matter" as privileging African Americans at the expense of everybody else, it is important to educate ourselves from the perspective of people who are included in the statement's meaning and what the movement aims to do. Meanwhile, Black Lives do Matter to us as Indigenous people, as all people and all of creation are to be respected. According to traditional Indigenous ethics, all play a role in our society and our global well-being. The widely used Lakota prayer statement "Mitakuye Oyasin" ("All My Relations") reminds us that all life is sacred.

We are also reminded by the premises of Indigenous restorative justice touched upon above that offenders are more than what they have done. They, along with their victims, must be made whole and reintegrated into our communities. Making each one whole again is a long, hard process. It will not get done through protests alone but will take many years of dedication to that task by all involved parties. We will all benefit from studying the tenets of Indigenous restorative justice and be ready to listen to all sides as equally worthy of our full attention.

It is very hard to reconcile both the knowledge of the abuses of the Jim Crow era and those of today with the need to respect all people regardless of ethnicity. This might explain the participation of many Lumbee in the anti-BLM crowds at the UNCP march. The history of Jim Crow policies that separated

American Indians in the South from all other groups is laid bare in the next three stories. Legal discrimination against people of color and the lumping of Native Americans into this murky racialist category allowed for the further erasure of Native American communities across the South. Native Americans in Virginia and South Carolina were not allowed separate categories in their states during Jim Crow. Native Americans in those states could not identify themselves or their children as Native American and were forced to go to Black or white schools depending on their skin color and the social norms of the communities. North Carolina allowed the Lumbee (in 1887) and later other North Carolina tribal communities to establish separate schools and identify as American Indian, but the state policies in North Carolina did not keep tribal citizens from the indignities of Jim Crow policies. Like American Indians in Virginia and South Carolina, North Carolina American Indians and African Americans were not allowed to eat in most restaurants, swim in public pools, shop in most stores, stay in most hotels, use white-only bathrooms or water fountains, be treated in many health clinics or doctor's offices, and on and on. Discrimination was legal and harshly enforced.

Kay Richardson Oxendine's story, "I Always Knew I Was Indian," recounts Kay's experiences of living in Richmond, Virginia, a major southern city where her parents moved the family for work. As a little girl, Kay learns to explain how she could be an Indian and still look different than her peers' stereotypes. She learns how to explain that she and her relations could all still exist despite her school's history lessons claiming that all Indians were dead. Kay's experience reflects the long-term effects of Virginia's Racial Integrity Law of 1924. The law stipulated that only two races—white and Black—were to be acknowledged in birth certificates and other official state documents. This legal practice constituted tribal genocide by bureaucracy. It is important to acknowledge that Richmond was the seat of the Confederacy. The tribal nations of Virginia had to fight long and hard to survive and regain legal recognition by the State of Virginia. Today, Virginia recognizes the tribal nations of the Chickahominy, Nansemond, Rappahannock, Mattaponi, Monacan, and Pamunkey communities.

Kay's experiences in Richmond, far from her tribal home in Hollister, North Carolina, gave her the courage and knowledge to write. Since childhood, she knew that her stories could serve to make sure that other little Native girls could know that it was not the words or actions of others that told you whether you were or were not Indian, but the relationships of your mother, father, uncles, aunties, and grandparents who told you who you were and what your tribe was about. Kay took a different path to justice that did not involve reconciliation with the children who bullied her or the lesson plans that erased her. She shaped justice for herself through her own determination to assure that other girls know their worth.

I also contributed the story about Uncle R. This is a family story that my cousins may recognize. The story is the inspiration for the title of this book section, "Getting Justice When There Was None." This story reflects the high value attached to revenge that is so central to the American version of justice familiar to all of us. My mother heard this story growing up, and she and her siblings knew their uncle well. They knew he was gentle even though his outward appearance did not reflect his true nature. While the motif of revenge is clearly visible in this narrative, Uncle R.'s story also reflects Indigenous restorative justice values. It holds that every person plays an important role in the community. Community members are valued as far more than the one bad thing they did or were alleged to have done.

The last essay in the book is based on an interview with Rosa Revels Winfree. Rosa Revels Winfree is the founder of the American Indian Women of Proud Nations Conference. She served as the organization's chair for many years until her health began to decline. The story tells of Rosa's experiences growing up, her journey into the outside world through her career in education, and her move to Charlotte, North Carolina, with her husband, Frank. Rosa Revels Winfree tells of hardships, of learning about non-Native people in negative and positive ways, and of recognizing her own prejudices and overcoming them. She recounts her teaching career's failures and triumphs as well as her work on the board of the National Indian Education Association (NIEA), the successful coordination of the NIEA national conference in Greensboro, North Carolina, and the creation of the American Indian Women of Proud Nations organization shortly afterward.

Rosa Revels Winfree worked tirelessly for Indian people in North Carolina and beyond. Her story belongs in the section about justice because even though she was never given some of the opportunities she sought, she continued to work toward her goals despite the obstacles of segregation and prejudice. She recognized that even though segregation was legal, it was not just or right.

FURTHER READING

Black Lives Matter, https://blacklivesmatter.com/.

Blu, Karen. *The Lumbee Problem: The Making of an American Indian People*. Lincoln: University of Nebraska Press, 2001 (originally published in 1980).

Gonzales, Angela, Judy Kertész, and Gabrielle Tayac. "Eugenics as Indian Removal: Sociohistorical Processes and the De(con)struction of American Indians in the Southeast." *The Public Historian* 29, no. 3 (2007): 53–67.

Gray, Barbara, and Pat Lauderdale. "The Great Circle of Justice: North American Indigenous Justice and Contemporary Restoration Programs." *Contemporary Justice Review* 10, no. 2 (2007): 215–25.

Jacobs, Mary Ann. "Southeastern American Indians, Segregation, and Historical Trauma Theory." In Cherry Maynor Beasley, Mary Ann Jacobs, and Ulrike Wiethaus, *American Indian Women of Proud Nations: Essays on History, Language, and Education,* 45–59. New York: Peter Lang Publishing, 2016.

Hand, Carol A., Judith Hankes, and Toni House. "Restorative Justice: The Indigenous Justice System." *Contemporary Justice Review* 15, no. 4 (2012): 449–67.

Metoui, Jessica. "Returning to the Circle: The Reemergence of Traditional Dispute Resolution in Native American Communities." *Journal of Dispute Resolution*, no. 2 (2007): 517–40.

U.S. Department of Justice. *Restorative Justice*. 1998. Retrieved on March 5, 2011, from https://www.ojp.gov/ncjrs/virtual-library /abstracts/restorative-justice-overview.

White Shield, Rosemary. "Healing Responses to Historical Trauma: Native Women's Perspectives." In Cherry Maynor Beasley, Mary Ann Jacobs, and Ulrike Wiethaus, *American Indian Women of Proud Nations: Essays on History, Language, and Education*, 23–45. New York: Peter Lang Publishing, 2016.

Patchwork Images

Images of the Native woman are engraved forever in our
    memories—
The faces, the names, the voices, the sounds and scents
Of the generations that came before us and
the vision of the generations that will follow.

Bonnets, tobacco fields, farming in early morning dew.
Canning butter beans, hog killings. Sunday school lessons.
Making a quilt for her children to fight over.

Studying her Bible, fixing homecoming dinner.
Nursing a baby, breaking a switch.
Hair turning gray, holding a grandchild.
These are the images of our women.

We can hear the humming of a sweet song that will last
Until her work is done. Amazing Grace.

Milk. Spit on a hankie. Wet biscuit dough on wet hands.
Fried fish. Fried chicken. Fried pork chops. Christmas cakes.
Turnips. Chicken and pastry.

Camay soap. Sweat. Jergen's lotion on Sunday morning.
These are the scents of our women.

These images can be heard, felt, seen, smelled, or tasted
In the communities where our Indian women live.

She is farmer, teacher, mother, factory worker,
Secretary, professional.

Her hair is tinted, gray, short, long.
She wears housecoats, britches,
Sunday dresses, power suits.
Her face is made more beautiful with cosmetics.
Her face is bare.
Her skin is soft. Her skin is weathered by years of
Struggle and tiny, tiny character lines frame her eyes.
She smells like French perfume.
She smells like Mother Earth.

The responsibility of being Native woman was placed upon
Her shoulders at her birth,
Blanketed—like a patchwork quilt—around her body.
The last generation (and the one before that) hover
Around her—protecting her from bad spirits.
The next generation (and the one after that) wait eagerly
for her to share the woman's secret of Creation.

Ruth Dial Woods

The Alcatraz Occupation and the Advent of Civil Rights and American Indian Nationalism

During the pre–civil rights decade, American Indians found themselves in increasing numbers finishing high school and entering college, partly because of relocation projects and later because of returning American Indian veterans from the Korean Conflict. In 1961, college students who attended the National Congress of American Indians meeting in Chicago expressed discontent with, but not disrespect for, their own organization and its apparent inertia. At a follow-up meeting, Stan Steiner reported that the purpose of the Red Power Indian Movement was to utilize the Indian students' university education to provide new Indian leadership to help their people back home and to promote Indian nationalism and cultural revivalism of pride in heritage, traditions, and culture. The Washington State Project and the Yakama Nation fish-ins helped fuel this incipient American Indian Movement. The 1964 Indian Self-Determination Act developed government programs and projects for Indian tribes, but the relocation projects created "cement prairies" and urban Indian ghettos. American Indian anger and protest became manifest in the Alcatraz Occupation in 1969 and 1970, the Wounded Knee Occupation in 1973, and the Longest Walk in 1978.

From November 1969 until June 1971, American Indians from across America as well as West Coast tribes occupied the Alcatraz Island and prison to draw attention to the poor conditions of Indian reservations across America and to establish a center for Native American studies as a call for renewal of Native culture and pride. Leaders of the occupation issued a national call for an American Indian Conference of All Tribes in December 1969 as a show of national unity.

THE AMERICAN INDIAN CENTER

On Monday, December 22, 1969, I left Fayetteville, North Carolina at 11:30 a.m. and flew by jet, arriving in San Francisco at 7:30 p.m. Shirley Keith, a worker at the American Indian Center in San Francisco, arranged to have someone meet me at the airport and take me to the center. Shirley was an outgoing person, an Indian woman full of vitality. I was nervous having never been that far from home, but as soon as I reached the center and met Shirley, I began to feel comfortable. It was heartwarming that first night to sit in the center until well after midnight and watch Indian people come and go in and out.

Funded by the Office of Economic Opportunity, the American Indian Center served as a Community Action Center, as we knew them in North Carolina. The interests of Indians were promoted by the presence of Indian staff in the center. Feeling welcome,

Indians could come and meet and share their ideas with people to whom they could relate. One woman and her husband came in looking for shirts for the husband. The couple rummaged through piles of clothing and boxes of junk for about two hours before the woman bagged up two large paper grocery bags of clothing and other items that she felt she could use.

Coffee was always brewing, and the center served as a mission where Indian people could find a comfortable place to visit and someone who could help them meet their immediate needs. From one man who came into the center for a cup of coffee, I learned that on many Indian reservations, the Bureau of Indian Affairs sponsored relocation projects that enticed Indians to leave the reservation and go to "the land of promise," that is, big cities where they could better their circumstances and find jobs, housing, and other services.

One relocatee, as they are called, sat in the center for three hours telling me of his disappointment. He had been led to believe that San Francisco could offer him everything. He had left his family because they could not relocate with him, come to the city, and enrolled in a training program but could get no permanent employment because he was an apprentice. He could not work long enough to save the money he needed to go back home to Pine Ridge Reservation in South Dakota and had to sleep in mission houses and overnight boarding houses. The relocation project offered grants of $1,700 to purchase homes; however, when an Indian reached a relocation area, the money failed to cover a down payment. As a result, relocatees had to incur debt to buy a decent place to live. Ultimately, Indian ghettos formed.

Substandard communities and housing became a way of life. Many were never able to get out of debt, their homes were confiscated, and they remained in the city unable to return to their home reservations.

ARE YOU INDIAN?

It was heartwarming to see the many people wander in and out of the center seeking tickets to board the boat to Alcatraz to join the protest and takeover of the island. They were convinced that the principle for which Alcatraz had been appropriated was a ray of hope for all Indian people. Having never experienced the dictatorship of the Bureau of Indian Affairs as these people had, I was puzzled but yet sympathetic with their hunger for return to their home reservations. Sometime after midnight, Shirley arranged for me to spend the night at the Chancellor House in downtown San Francisco so that I could get to the dock the next morning and return midday to get back to the airport without great difficulty. On Tuesday morning, I got up at 6:00 a.m. to board the boat to the island. I rode the cable car from the hotel and was able to view Chinatown on my way. I walked three blocks from the end of the cable line down to Fisherman's Wharf where I was to board. Imagine San Francisco Bay at 7:00 a.m. in misty rain and smog with the smell of fish, crabs, and shrimp being cooked in sidewalk restaurants along the pier. Many of us have smelled such aromas at the beach, but in San Francisco (and I understand this is true in Japan and other fishing countries), they begin early in the morning cooking seafood on the sidewalks to sell throughout the day.

I walked about four or five blocks trying to find Pier Number 47. When I found it, I met about ten other Indians waiting to board the small fishing boat that left every twenty minutes for the island. A small pickup truck gate spread over with a canvas was the waiting place for boarding. When I approached the truck, I was asked to sign my name, tribe, and address. Two weeks earlier, the Alcatraz Tribal Council had decided that anyone with less than three quarters Indian blood would be excluded from the island. A young Indian girl looked at me hard and asked, "Are you Indian?" I replied, "Yes." Then she asked, "What tribe?" When I responded "Lumbee," the expression on her face showed her doubts of the existence of such a tribe. I pulled out my North Carolina driver's license that identified me as Indian, and reluctantly, ever so reluctantly, she agreed to let me sign in and book.

As I waited to board the boat, several other groups arrived—single women and men, children, and families. Some had come, as I had, just for this purpose. The boat carried only twenty-seven people at a time, but each time it was filled to capacity.

I met a Lakota family from South Dakota—a mother, father, three married daughters, and two sons-in-law—who were going to the island for the American Indian Conference of All Tribes. I was impressed with the family, and we became close friends for the next few hours. I noted the strong familial ties—Indian ties—of this family who had come to spend Christmas on Alcatraz. Our fishing boat docked beside a barge on the island. All the federal signs had been painted over. One sign that faintly read, US Government Property—Keep Out had been painted over to read INDIAN PROPERTY—INDIANS WELCOME! Also,

Alcatraz Island read INDIAN LAND. These were the same signs that I had seen on television about the Alcatraz Occupation. The media blitz told the nation of the illegal takeover of the federal prison that had long been vacated and was no longer operated by the United States government, but what the media did not tell the nation was the reason for the occupation and national protest.

STEPPING OFF THE BOAT

I can scarcely describe my mixed feelings when a security guard met me as I stepped off the boat. No one could get on the island without being screened by this security guard, and you could not proceed without a guide. Members of the security guard were stationed at strategic points on the island and were assigned to keep watch on a schedule. On the flagpole flew a red-and-white-striped flag with an eagle in the place of the stars. My first impression was that of being in a foreign land, but soon I felt a part of the common cause that had brought me here in the first place. Beginning at the landing point, I ascended a circular road to the top of the island and the central prison where the conference was to be held.

When we entered the prison building, we had once again to sign a register that indicated name, tribe, address, and group being represented. After registration, we were led down the rows of prison cells, all dusty, bleak, and gray with cold concrete and steel bars.

The meeting was in the dining hall, where the only heat came from small portable gas burners that were also used for cooking.

All the food had been brought from the mainland. Each time a family occupied the island, they had to register and be assigned a specific detail like cooking, housekeeping, nursery attendance, teaching the schoolchildren, or maintaining security. Each new person planning to stay on the island was required to take a medical examination. Rules and regulations were passed along to visitors and new residents, and the security guards enforced them strictly. The original conveners of the protest managed to organize an efficient working crew under stressful circumstances.

A CHEYENNE WOMAN'S STORY

My blanket and my clothes became soaked from the continual drizzle while I rode the boat from the dock and walked onto the "Rock." With little heat inside, I remained wrapped in the blanket. A Cheyenne woman took pity and offered me an extra dry blanket she had brought with her. Her son had been on the island for two weeks, and she came from thirty miles north of San Francisco every chance she got to participate in the protest. I pause here to recall her story.

At the age of nine, she had been taken away from her family on the reservation and sent five hundred miles away from her home reservation to a Bureau of Indian Affairs boarding school in New Mexico. She had never had an opportunity to share in any kind of family life with her aunts, uncles, cousins, and grandparents. When she finished high school, she came to California where her brother had relocated through a BIA project. She had been reared in another culture and felt (as many of us do) that she had been deprived of the knowledge of her Native culture. She married an Italian but had never been accepted in the Italian community. She mentioned that she had called her neighbors and tried to solicit food, clothing, and blankets for the people on Alcatraz but received absolutely no help. She was young, about thirty-eight, attractive, and searching (like me) for a common bond with Indian people.

I found it difficult to imagine having my children taken from me and sent away, but others have told me that this is the way of life for many tribes on the reservations. An elderly Lakota gentleman expressed a negative attitude toward education because of the way the government had forced education upon Indian people. He spoke of the school he was forced to attend and the punishment he received there. He said the Indian headmaster who worked for the BIA had been more interested in his job and pleasing the BIA than in the well-being and education of young Indian people.

REBELS WITH A CAUSE

After a call to conference by Richard Oakes, Mohawk from New York State and tribal chair of the Alcatraz Occupation, workshops were announced, and everyone was encouraged to select one workshop. The workshops addressed operational aspects of establishing a National Native American Center on Alcatraz to promote national awareness of Native American culture and the plight of the American Indian. All moderators and panelists were Indian, and a Tribal Council Steering Committee comprised of the Indians who had originally occupied the island in

November 1969 led the conference. Aubrey Grossman discussed legal issues that dealt with treaty rights, historical land grants, and treaties that had disposed of California lands, and the necessity to focus on sovereignty over legal technicalities related to the occupation. Earl Livermore, a Blackfoot and former director of the San Francisco American Indian Center, served as conference coordinator.

Other workshops focused on how to raise funds to maintain the protest and Indian presence on the island. The duties and responsibilities of the Tribal Council Steering Committee were discussed and staff introduced to the assembly. An architectural drawing of proposed divisions within the building and design and layout for center operations had been drawn, and copies were presented to all in attendance. Admissions and qualifications standards had been developed by the Tribal Council to determine the eligibility and approval of individuals and families who would occupy the island and assist with the activities and programs envisioned for the center.

I would describe the Tribal Council as an activist group, militantly dedicated to the development of an awareness of Indian concerns and discontent. These young Indian students were ready, with fortitude and conviction, to endanger their lives to bring the problems of Indians into the national limelight. Families were occupying the island with their children with no heat, with a limited food supply, and in uncomfortable living conditions. These were truly "rebels with a cause" that I could easily endorse and support in the same spirit of dedication and commitment evident in the faces of the four hundred Indians who had come together on Alcatraz Island on Tuesday, December 23, 1969.

We often speak of pride, and this was a prime example of group pride. It was an awesome experience to feel the commonality of principle and conviction permeating the meetings. It was both interesting and gratifying to note that the Tribal Council had prepared a map and included location points of all Indian tribes in the United States, Canada, and Mexico. I pointed with pride at the "Lumbee" mark in North Carolina and knew then that other Indians knew of us, although the woman at the gate had never heard of the Lumbee.

A Choctaw woman heard that I was from Pembroke and asked about our famous rout of the Ku Klux Klan. Marie Potts, who spoke on television later that evening on the mainland, came up and asked about Judge Lacy Maynor and his daughter, Helen Schierbeck, who had been my childhood playmate and schoolmate. I felt myself a part of this great event because these were my friends—my people. While I felt uncomfortable climbing rope ladders on and off fishing boats, it was only fitting that I did so as I witnessed many elderly persons—women and men, gray-haired and disabled—climbing the same rope ladders. The mixture of old and young filled with hope and firm in their convictions and commitment to Indian people was an impressive sight and a wonderful moment.

FEELING THE FLOW OF SPIRIT

After the meetings on Tuesday night, the Los Angeles Indian Dancers arrived to hold a powwow. Such an array of regalia and dances must have projected light all the way to the mainland. With next to no heat and only emergency electricity from a generator (the government caretaker had pulled all the electrical circuits), the closeness and camaraderie at the end of this day filled me with warmth. All the cold and dampness faded as I shared in these events. I regretted that I could spend so little time getting to know the people better. I felt the flow of spirit, and I saw friends in the faces of those around. I felt for the first time in my life a true bond of Indian kinship. How fortunate many of us have been in many ways, but how we have been robbed of our heritage. I see nothing fortunate in becoming "White Man's Indians" as compared to those Indians who value a sense of kinship and bond of humanity amid barriers few of us could overcome alone. I feel inherent and innate values still within us that, coupled with a new awareness of Indian culture and pride, could make us stronger as a people.

These thoughts struck me as I boarded the small fishing boat late that evening and looked back at the dim lights on Alcatraz Island. I had spent approximately twenty hours in the center and on the island, another world, but a world with great attraction for me personally. I could welcome the comfort of heat and warmth in a hotel room, but I knew that the spirit and communion I had felt on Alcatraz Island would make me a better person. I left this new world sadly, and I knew I had to return. But I also knew I had gained knowledge that I could share. I felt close to the Indians of Alcatraz, and I knew I had been filled with pride being able to relate to my Indian brothers and sisters in ways I had never known. I will never forget suffering in the cold and damp dining hall and looking out the window at the children playing in heavy blowing rains. I was freezing, yet they were happy to play in an atmosphere of freedom and with Indian pride and self-confidence. I still see the faces of those who sat intently and deeply engrossed in the struggle for Alcatraz and the greater principle it represented for all of us.

I departed San Francisco on Wednesday morning, December 24, 1969, and arrived in Fayetteville late in the afternoon, but still in time to celebrate Christmas Eve. Although tired and weary, I was more knowledgeable and ready to reaffirm my commitment to the struggle.

Flora Jacobs and Mary Ann Jacobs

"This is something I am really glad to participate in"

TWO GENERATIONS REFLECT ON THE BLACK LIVES MATTER MOVEMENT

FLORA'S PERSPECTIVE

My name is Flora Jacobs. I am an enrolled member of the Lumbee Tribe. I live in Pembroke, a small university town in Robeson County, North Carolina. I am twenty-two years old and a graduate of the Massage Therapy and Bodyworks Program at Robeson Community College. I am studying to take my exam for certification. This is my story of "Getting Justice When There Was None."

On Friday, June 26, 2020, a march dedicated to the Black Lives Matter movement was held in Pembroke, North Carolina, the heart of the Lumbee homeland. It was organized by a group of university students, including student government and Black Greeks. I protested in that march alongside my mother, Mary Ann Jacobs. On that Friday evening at 5:00 p.m., my mother and I walked to the Jones Center on the campus of the University of North Carolina at Pembroke (UNCP) and joined a group of people gathering for the march. It included members of UNCP student organizations, other students, staff, faculty, and townspeople. We all gathered with the same intentions and understanding. We wanted to show our disappointment and express that we stand against police brutality and racism. We arrived ready to support the march with homemade signs, posters, clothing, masks, and flags. There was so much creativity and representation put into the pieces we wore, wrote, designed, and presented. It was wonderful to see this amount of care come from the community.

"SAY THEIR NAMES"

All over the world, and continuing to the present day, protests, marches, and riots take place in the name of the Black Lives Matter movement. The United States has been struggling particularly hard with its deeply rooted racism for centuries. Too many events involving police brutality end in the deaths of African Americans. This carelessness, inhumanity, hate, physical force, racism, and injustice was the brew that was boiling to cause this movement's time of unrest. At the same time, we find ourselves in the middle of a pandemic unlike anything since the 1912 Spanish influenza epidemic.

Alicia Garza, Opal Tometi, and Patrisse Cullors created the Black Lives Matter movement on July 13, 2013. The movement campaigns against white supremacy in all its forms, systemic racism, violence against Black people, and police brutality. When Trayvon Martin died on February 26, 2012, at the hands of George Zimmerman, a white male living in Sanford, Florida, his death brought about a national response so great that it led to the creation of this powerful movement. Many more deaths were to be added to a list under the powerful statement "Say Their Names." People such as Anthony McClain, Rayshard Brooks, George Floyd, Breonna Taylor, John Neville, Jordan Edwards, Riah Milton, and Dominique "Rem'mie" Fells are just a few of the many names on that list. The people commemorated ranged from young to old, from male to female, and some are from the LGBTQ+ community.[1]

One of the most jarring events connected with the Black Lives Matter movement was the murder of George Floyd. When officers responded to a report of forgery at 3759 Ave South in Minneapolis, Minnesota, things became lethal very quickly. A bystander caught the horrid chain of events on video. George Floyd was physically restrained after being asked to get out of his vehicle. A police officer by the name of Derek Chauvin was seen in the video placing his knee on George's neck as George is pinned down and held in a vulnerable position. Floyd says multiple times, "I can't breathe." The officer ignores his pleas. Floyd eventually loses consciousness and is taken to Hennepin County Medical Center where he later died.

When my mother and I got to the Jones Center, the students had set up a table with water, Gatorade, and some snacks for the protestors. It was very hot outside that day, and the sky was a very pretty blue. We waited about an hour for more people to join our group. People of all ethnicities were coming together that day to march. I remember thinking to myself, "This is something I am really glad to participate in here today." When the time came for us to start, which was around 6:00 p.m., the leaders of the

1. https://blacklivesmatter.com/. Accessed December 15, 2020.

march (the student organizers) thanked us for coming out and supporting the cause. When we first arrived, we noticed that a few police officers from the town's police station were there with us. We were told that the march was planned with the police so that we could protest peacefully. The police escort was intended to help keep us safe. We recited a few of our chants such as "No Justice, No Peace," "Black Lives Matter," and "I Can't Breathe." We were to walk through campus toward the center of town. We did not know what to expect during this march.

"WE DON'T NEED YOU IN OUR TOWN."

News of this peaceful protest had spread all over social media on places like Facebook and Twitter. There were many mixed reactions. I saw plenty of negative feedback. People wrote that they needed to "protect their town from looting or the destroying of property." From our vantage point, that was not going to happen at all. I thought the fear was ridiculous. Others were vocal about their point of view on the Black Lives Matter movement, whether critical or supportive.

Our group had grown. We were about 150, perhaps even 200 people strong. We started the walk from the Jones Center, then moved past the Chavis Center toward the newly built welcoming university sign. We were about three blocks into our march when we stopped in front of the Burger King past our campus. A local preacher offered to say a prayer with us before we walked more deeply into town. Everyone took a knee. We bowed our heads as we listened to his prayer. After we stood up, I noticed an older woman. She was holding a sign of her own as she was standing near the front of the group. It was a Trump 2020 poster. It included a photograph of President Trump. She was repeating the phrase "Natives for Trump."

We continued to march on the main road's sidewalk, which cuts through the town of Pembroke. We had gained more people marching with us since we left campus. We soon saw numerous townspeople gathered on the other side of the street. Traffic on the road was full of cars. Due to the police escort, the passing cars slowed down and observed us walking on one side of the street and the opposing side responding to our march on the other side. As we chanted the phrases we had practiced before we started walking, we were met with opposing chants such as "All Lives Matter," "Native Lives Matter," and "Go Home." I also heard other statements such as "We don't need you in our town," "We won't let you loot our stores," and often, vulgar words, including the N-word as well.

From the crowd of people yelling at us from the other side of the road, I was really surprised to see some people I recognized, even people I went to school with. That made me feel disappointed. Yet there was also a little support from others. Kind words such as "We are with you," and "Thank you for standing up for what is right." It was a lot to take in. All the cars, the shouting, the hate, all the eyes on you from all the people. Usually, you do not see that many people on the streets of Pembroke unless the Christmas or Homecoming Parades are happening. Pembroke may be a small town, but still, it is home to many, many people.

We walked about a mile to the center of town. In front of the shops that run down the center's block, a storeowner was kind enough to pass out water bottles from her store entrance for those of us who needed a drink. We took time to listen to a few of the participants who had walked with us. They discussed the importance of our protest in Pembroke. We were reminded that we did not need to listen to the degrading words of the counterprotesters. We were marching to represent the lives of Black Americans, the #BLM movement, justice, and equality in such a horrible world as ours. I took the time to film the speeches via Facebook Live on my cell phone.

NAME-CALLING AND CURSING

After the speeches, we retraced our steps back through town. About that time, a man on his motorcycle rode through town alongside us. He started revving his engine every time we would start a chant. I noticed he had a smirk on his face as he was revving up his bike to try to silence our voices. It was aggravating, especially because I was walking on the sidewalk beside the road. He was riding very close to me, so it was very loud. His interference did not discourage anyone from chanting and marching on.

We were close to campus when things took a turn. There was a man on the opposing side of the road from us. He was wearing his rifle strapped to his chest, shouting threats at us. Someone else had decided to start throwing beer bottles, and one man threw a water bottle from which he had been drinking. The name-calling and the cursing continued as well. A few more angry men decided to start walking toward us, threatening to harm some of our protestors. By now, most of the car traffic dividing our group from the counterprotesters was gone. They started toward us, crossing the street. Police officers had to intervene to keep them from laying hands on anyone. A few of the protesters we were walking with were getting angry and yelling back at the threatening men. Leaders of the protest as well as fellow protesters had to remind them that we needed to march on and not respond to the racism and hate with any anger.

The situation relaxed when we got back to campus. We gathered back at the Jones Center. Everyone was able to settle down. We gathered in a circle and listened to the protest leaders. They thanked us for coming and supporting the march. They reminded us that we needed to vote in the upcoming election, as well as in future elections within the state and city, regionally as well as nationally.

A GROWING BACKLASH

Over the next few days, official responses to the protest were issued from the Lumbee Tribal Office, the UNCP administration, the town of Pembroke, and a few news outlets. An almost week-long curfew was put in effect for the town in reaction to online responses on social media. It seemed that the backlash was growing. Marches and protests were prohibited. Recorded footage of what we endured while marching was posted online so that those who were not there could see what had happened. A sea of support emerged from people who saw the hate. They responded with words of support and care.

This experience opened our eyes as a Native community. We saw our own people react to a movement in support of other people of color in a bad way. Considering our shared history, the backlash is especially dreadful. For centuries, both Lumbee

Natives and African American people have endured slavery, rape, murder, torture, segregation, racism, and hate. We have common ground in a history of violence and oppression. For this reason, it does not make sense to see so many people in our community act this way about a Black Lives Matter protest. I have personally heard before from some Lumbee people that "we are better than Black folk." That is just not true. We are not better than anyone else. We are not above anyone. We are all human. We are all people with thoughts, emotions, and souls. We cannot keep treating each other differently just because of the color of our skin. This deeply rooted racial problem is dividing a tribal community as much as it divides a nation. It is not too far off to say that it is dividing the world as a whole, because racism is everywhere. It is being magnified in the United States right now because of our different moral and political beliefs, and because of how we look physically. Police brutality is not necessary. It is not humane, right, or even politically correct. It needs to end. There are many good police officers, but it seems that there are more bad ones.

It is going to take a long time to fix this broken system. If given the opportunity to attend more BLM protests and protests against the police brutality that is too rampant in this country, I will most definitely be attending them.

MARY ANN'S PERSPECTIVE

My daughter wanted to join the march and support the protesters because she saw similar marches on Facebook "blow up" before. I went to support my students. I believe a teacher's place is with their students. As Flora notes, we went to campus early on the day of the protest. We did not yet see the opposing crowd gathering in downtown Pembroke or the police staffing the route of the march. At our point of departure, people of all ethnic backgrounds had gathered with homemade signs that said Black Lives Matter, Jesus Protested, Racism is a Pure Arnt Shame!, End Police Brutality, and Breanna Taylor, George Floyd, Michael Brown, Alan Sterling, Sandra Bland . . . & So Many More!!!, No Justice, No Peace. The signs were not elaborate, but they were creative. We were instructed to only listen to the protest leaders and not to respond to the opposing crowd. It was a beautiful hot day. Some of the clouds in the sky were small and fluffy. Most were just smudges of white as if they had been rubbed out and spread across the blue of the sky.

THE ANGRY CROWD

The march started. We walked across the parking lots to the campus gateway at the traffic circle. There was no hint of rain, and the humidity was nonexistent. It was a truly rare June day at the beginning of a Robeson County summer. We crossed the railroad tracks that separate town from campus. We could finally see the opposing crowd gathered across the street from us on the opposite sidewalk. There were also people casually riding through town, which made it appear as if it was a Friday or Saturday night. Traffic was backing up. At the corner, we knelt with Rev. Dr. Mike Cummings who asked for permission to address us. He prayed with us. We stopped there for just a moment that felt good and that was indeed good. Only one short moment later, we saw the opposing crowd stretching all the way down the street and along our march's path.

The angry crowd was far bigger than the number of #BLM marchers. We were walking and shouting phrases such as "Black Lives Matter" and "No Justice No Peace." On the other side of the street, counterdemonstrators were yelling "All Lives Matter" and "Trump 2020" when they were not cursing at us and calling us the N-word. Most of the opposing crowd and those cruising through on their cars appeared to be fellow Lumbee. The crowds driving through town on the street between us seemed to expect to see the police tear-gassing the protesters, or looting, or some other mayhem. They had their phones out to capture whatever happened as they drove by us in slow motion. The march proceeded as peacefully as planned. The cruisers did not get to see any mobs of demonstrators looting, or the police teargassing us or any other Black and Brown bodies. It was among the opposing crowds where the violence took place.

The counterdemonstrators tried their best to drown out our voices as we marched toward downtown. The occasional motorcycle rider would drive through the street and slow down beside us to muffle our voices by revving up their engines. Counterdemonstrators were yelling at us the entire way. As Flora notes, some held All Lives Matter signs and Natives for Trump signs or waved Trump 2020 flags. In contrast, none of the BLM marchers had any Biden signs. Some of the BLM marchers chanted "All Lives Won't Matter Until Black Lives Matter." One BLM marcher shouted out to the opposing crowd "We love you!" and "Thanks for your support!" One of the Lumbee business owners passed us cold water bottles as we passed her shop. In contrast, someone from the opposing crowd threw water bottles and nearly full beer cans at us as we marched. I stepped over a can of beer as its contents spilled out over the sidewalk. Across the street, we could see one man with an assault rifle in a sling on his shoulder. He was short and the gun stretched down to his ankles. I found out later that he was non-Native from out of town.

Campus and town police escorted us the entire way. There were also plain-clothed individuals; maybe they were police officers, too. Our university chancellor, who recently had undergone foot surgery, rode in a golf cart at the end of the march. When we reached our destination at the UNCP Business Incubator building, we turned off Main Street to pause for brief speeches and prayers. Afterward, we turned the corner again to walk back to campus. At every step we took, the opposing crowd acted as described. We marchers kept moving and shouting, "Black Lives Matter!" and "No Justice, No Peace!"

WHAT HAD I JUST SEEN?

When we reached campus, we gathered one more time in the parking lot where we started. The student leaders asked those gathered not to be discouraged and encouraged fellow students to get involved in student government and campus organizations, to register to vote, and to actually vote. No one mentioned the opposing crowd or what we had just gone through together. The march seemed to end quickly, and with little fanfare. Everyone was exhausted. We all went home.

After the march, I can recall feeling numb and wondering what I had just experienced. What had I just seen? I had no idea why I viewed a Black Lives Matter march so differently from the other people across the street. I saw an opportunity to go to my daughter's first protest march. I saw students from my school learning to exercise their constitutional right to speak and think freely about a justice system that creates and condones what seems like an endless stream of Black people being killed by police. To what destination, I asked myself, is that blood flowing? Instead of a river moving to the ocean, that stream of blood has spread out across our lands. Do we not all hear the voice of our brothers' and sisters' blood crying out to us from the ground?

I marched with my daughter not because I was scared for her safety or for what she might see, but because I wanted her to be able to know that she could speak, march, protest, shout, and support people regardless of whether they were Lumbee, Tuscarora, Black, Asian, Latinx, Anglo, queer, straight, poor, sick, broken, or well. That day a rainbow of people marched in the BLM march in Pembroke. We marchers were the rainbow that reminds us of a promise. The promise that we are all worthy of God's love and that we are all responsible for allowing that love to shine out through us.

I Always Knew I Was Indian

I always knew I was Indian. I was that kid who always asked questions. Some questions Mom and Dad could not answer. They tried to give me the blanket answers, but I always pulled back the covers and asked more. I was the baby of three and carried the burden that Mommy almost died having me (heard this story since the day I was born!). My sister and brother used this as leverage, so yeah, I got picked on, a lot! But I tell you, if someone would have told me that I would be a business owner when I was a little girl, I would have laughed. Moving to Richmond from Hollister was my mom and dad's idea to better their lives. In doing so, we were also exposed to things that not even my mom and dad had ever seen. Discrimination and hatred were part of our everyday schedules. My dad spoke to me about having to enter the back door to many restaurants because of his tan skin.

We were so dirt poor! We lived on Oregon Hill, which was a rough neighborhood in the city of Richmond. We had so many roaches and bugs in our row house that I thought that roaches had their own whole communities and held local news conferences, warning them where Raid was used. They wore suits, ties, and glasses and ate dinner at tables like us. Our human neighbors consisted of families with children, alcoholics, hippies, and old folks. We lived on the 700 block of Pine Street, and my brother, sister, and I walked eight blocks to the St. Andrews private school. Our neighborhood was on the news almost every evening, but never for good reasons.

During my childhood, hearing screams, seeing flashing lights, and avoiding child abductors or molesters was a normal routine. There were so many sirens at night that we became immune to them. One night in particular, we heard screams, and my sister and I just lay there staring out our back window that faced the alley. The next morning, we learned that a young girl had been raped and her throat slit, right in our back alley. When I got older, I learned that there had been a serial rapist during that time, and most of his victims were found in Hollywood Cemetery, which was on the back end of our neighborhood, about six blocks up and three blocks over. Mom tried to shield us from bad things, but when it happens in your back alley, you have got to kind of tell your kids what was up.

HEY, DO YOU WANT SOME ICE CREAM?

My brother, who was only two and a half years older than me, was my sister's and my protector. He would walk with us to school and would "man up" if needed. Because Mom and Dad needed to work, my brother was our "adult" who would take care of us for the few hours before Mom and Dad came home. He was nine years old.

One day, this was much needed as my sister and I were approached by a white man who slowed down his vehicle and began speaking to me and my sis. Me being the outgoing one, I was like, "Hi!"

He said, "Hey, you want some ice cream?"

I was like, "Really?"

He said, "Yeah, come on with me."

I walked toward him, and my brother was like, "Wait, who are you?"

The man said, "A friend of your dad."

My brother said, "I have never seen you before."

I stopped just a few feet away from his car. He opened his door and was like, "Come on, little girl. I will give you ice cream."

I immediately knew that if he were my dad's friend, he would have known my name, so I turned and ran, dropping my books in the street. My brother and sister ran after me, and as soon as we got home, we called Mom and told her what happened. She told us to lock the door and wait for them to come home. One of our neighbors on the 600 block saw what had happened and brought me my books and told us we did the right thing. Later that week, the news announced that a young girl had been abducted in our neighborhood. A profile of the man was on the news, and I told Mom that sounded like the man who had talked to us. We gave extra praise that night before we ate dinner for that little girl being found and the fact that we were safe.

ADOPTING A FAMILY FOR CHRISTMAS

Mom worked at night so that Daddy could attend college. When we lived on Oregon Hill, Mom and Dad reached out to strangers, because they were afraid we would not have a Christmas. Being a little girl of four, it made no sense to me when a strange white woman came to my home and gave me a white baby doll. First off, I did not know her. Second, it was not Santa or my mom giving me the doll. And third, who was this woman? I never played with that doll, but that memory ended up framing my adult life in how I gave back to the community. When I began my work life, an opportunity came to join a volunteer organization. I jumped at it, and our first project was adopting a family for Christmas. One of the leaders was the one who organized the first drop to our selected family. I listened as she criticized the family she had just given Christmas to. She made notice that the husband had a beer and was standing in the yard. She noticed how the family had a large TV. She noticed how the children were clean and their clothes were nice. She said if they were so poor, how could that man stand in the yard, how could the kids look so nice, and how could they afford that nice TV? For the next family, I went grocery shopping with her and again learned the absolute horror of white privilege. She bought the families bent cans, saying that they were lucky to have these foods. She bought the bargain brands and powdered milk. She insisted again that these people were lucky to have anything! With the toy drive, she accepted hand-me-down toys and secondhand clothes, many with holes and tears.

The next year, I was named the volunteer coordinator, and I changed all the rules.

First, I made sure it was adapted into our laws that when we select our families, it is *none of our business* why they are being adopted. The fact that they asked was enough; it was not up to us to judge. I encouraged the group to go through Social Services instead of us personally delivering the goods because that way, the integrity of familiar relationships was kept in place with the children, and the embarrassment that may come from strangers coming to their home was erased. When we went for groceries, I made sure that the families not only got the brand names, but we also purchased a fresh turkey, a gallon of milk, real butter, and a dozen eggs. I imagined what I would want for a holiday meal, and that is what they got as well. When it came to toys, I sent messages out company-wide that we needed new toys or gently used ones. I wanted to be sure that when a little girl or boy came to the tree on Christmas morning, their dream of Santa would still be in place, and their moms and dads would still be their heroes. I never wanted anyone to feel the way I felt when that woman handed me that doll so many years ago.

THE SOUTHSIDE OF RICHMOND

Another pivotal point that affected my childhood was when my family decided to move to the Southside of Richmond. It was the promise of a new land! It was Mom and Dad's first (and only) home they purchased. And we were the first dark people to move to Davey Gardens. At first, the racism was disguised as curiosity. *Where are you from?* To which I would answer, *Oregon Hill.* That wasn't the right answer. So, they went on. *I mean, what are you?* I said, *A girl.*

I truly had no idea what they were talking about. And then, the neighborhood bully came and brought friends, and they circled my little bike. *You're a N——! We don't want you here!* They chased me on my bike, and I was pedaling hard! They kept catching up with me and holding my seat bar and kept surrounding me. But I made it to my road, and kept turning around and defending myself, saying, *I am not a N——! I am half Indian!* The kids said, *Same thing*, and continued to try to beat on me. My dad heard the ruckus and came and stood on the porch. With this turn of events, they released me, and I pedaled home. When I walked into the door, Daddy asked me what that was about. I told them they were calling me N—— . . . "And I said I am not a N—— . . . I am half Indian." My daddy's expression was priceless, and before I knew it, there was a hand across my face!

"*What?* Why did you say that, Kay? You are *only* Indian! If you tell folks that you are half anything, what do you think they think the other half is? Do you have any idea what is running through your veins?"

I was crying and was like, "Well, no!"

Daddy sat me down and expressed how both he and mom were Indian from the same tribe. He said, "How come you didn't know that?" I told him it was because in history they told me all Indians were dead.

THE WORK IS NONSTOP

Thus began my writing career. I wrote my first book in fifth grade, telling the world about my tribe. I asked my mom and dad, my grandmothers and grandfather. I asked my great-grandma Roxie. I asked my uncles and aunts. I talked to the tribal historians. I wrote and wrote and wrote about Indian people. I never ever wanted another young girl to think all Indians were dead, especially if she was one. I had radio programs where I talked about Indian people. I was the founder and president of the Virginia Native American Cultural Center, Inc. (VNACC), which formed in 1991. I became the extras casting associate for *The*

Broken Chain (Lamont Johnson, dir., 1993), and it was my job to find the Indians for the movie. I did. I became the senior moderator on Powwows.com to educate folks. I partnered with Barry Richardson on Pow-wows, Inc. and became his public relations person, work which I still do. I worked as an editor for the *Country Courier* when I realized that in a community that was rich in Native culture, there was no Native news. I made sure that Native people were in every issue. After leaving there, I started my own newspaper, *360 Connection*. When the publisher decided to leave, within a week I started another newspaper entitled *360 View*. After closing this paper, I began writing for *Native Hoop Magazine*, where I have now been named associate editor. I am one of the founding members of the *Women's Sacred River Drum Society* and have been emceeing powwows in the last five years, which is a predominantly male role. I also make sure I take plenty of pictures at every cultural event I go to and post them on my Facebook page so that the whole world can continue to visualize the richness and strength of our people. The work is nonstop, and I find myself repeating my story almost daily. But it is all worth it.

Mary Ann Jacobs

Uncle R. Never Killed Nobody That Didn't Deserve It

LISTENING TO THE GROWN-UPS TALK

When I was young, my family lived in Chicago, but our parents usually took summer vacations in Pembroke, North Carolina. When our families would gather, I used to love sitting with the adults while they would talk. Late in the evenings my mother and father's siblings, their spouses, and their parents would gather for long family meals. After dinner, the kids would run outside for endless tag games through my paternal grandfather's farm and similar games at my mother's sisters' homes. The adults would gather on the screened porch or in the yard. Wherever we went, my parents and my aunts and uncles became storytellers as they caught up with family goings-on. I loved to play with the kids, but I also loved to sit and listen to the grown-ups talk. The past was never far from these discussions, as the past was always a lesson for what was happening currently, and it was a source of comfort and pride for my relatives. I never really understood most of these stories that my relatives would discuss. They included a lot of insider information that I could not decipher at the time; they also included lots of grown-up information about my Lumbee relatives who had passed on long ago.

There were lots of these types of stories about my mother's Uncle R. My mother's siblings and their spouses always called him Uncle R., so we kids called him that, too, even though we children were all one generation removed from this uncle. As a child, I heard stories that Uncle R. had walked to Georgia from Pembroke "just to kill a man" and turned around to walk back when the task was done. Other stories held that Uncle R. killed at least two men and that the local sheriff was afraid to arrest him. The story went that the sheriff went to Uncle R.'s house to arrest him but called out to Uncle R. from the safety of his station wagon instead of taking him forcibly from his home. The sheriff yelled to Uncle R., "Come-on now R., you know why I'm here."

And Uncle R. replied, "I ain't goin' nowhere with you!"

Apparently, this single exchange was enough to make the sheriff leave and never return. At least, that's how the story went.

There may have been other times when the sheriff came for Uncle R., but this was "the Sheriff and Uncle R." story that I heard many times. There were other stories including details such as that Uncle R. talked to himself all the time, especially when he had been drinking. He also always carried long sharp machetes with him wherever he went. When these stories were retold, the adults were always careful to say that "Uncle R. never killed nobody that didn't deserve it." I thought that was particularly funny, but I didn't know why it was an important part of the story.

THE ADULT PART OF THE STORY

As I stated previously, growing up I did not know the whole story of Uncle R., and I would not learn the fuller version of the story until I was an adult. The adult part of the story was part of the insider information that I was too young to learn about during those summer evening chats. Instead, my mother and her family would exchange the bits and pieces of the larger Uncle R. story that could be shared in the presence of children. Back then, I never questioned why my mother's relatives would share stories about someone who may have been a murderer, drank a lot, and had such a violent life that he constantly carried weapons. As a child hearing these stories, they just sounded like exciting tales about someone who was kind of "not real" in his ability to fend off annoying people and kill those that deserved it all while avoiding any punishment. All I knew was that Uncle R. did not tolerate anybody trying to "mess" with him, but I didn't know why my relatives thought these stories were okay to repeat in front of children or why these were the stories that were so often repeated.

You have to understand that most Lumbee family gatherings are not a time to sit around and tell traditional myth or creation stories the way other tribal people might. Those tellings often share a story with lessons about how one is supposed to act in challenging times in one's life. Instead, our Lumbee stories are about real people in our families. These stories are our family lore, but none of it is mythical to us. As a child and young adult, it never occurred to me that the Uncle R. stories were teaching lessons for Lumbee children and adults. The stories always include information about your kin and how you are related to certain families or individuals. That is why they were so enduring in my family.

As an adult, I was finally old enough to understand how inappropriate all those Uncle R. stories were for children, and I slowly started asking questions about Uncle R. When I was young and overhearing these stories, I did not get to interrupt the adult conversations, because I really was not supposed to be sitting there listening in the first place. I was supposed to be out playing with my siblings and cousins in the yard or fields. On the occasions when we were allowed to stay close by, it was okay for a child to sit with the adults and listen, but it was not okay to ask annoying questions. The adults moved swiftly from one topic (or story) to the next. They did not have time to stop and explain, especially if it was not a story that was polite to be discussing in front of a child. That type of questioning might make someone ask you, "Shouldn't you be outside playing with the other children?" That would be your invitation to leave.

AN IMPORTANT PERSON IN ROBESON COUNTY

As an adult, I finally learned the adult version of the Uncle R. stories over time, and through asking the questions that never seemed to occur to me as a child. I finally learned that Uncle R. was an important person in Robeson County. He had a specific job that people valued. He was kind and loved children. He was a single parent who was providing for his children after his wife, the love of his life, died. Uncle R. did not always drink. He became an alcoholic after his wife died. A man broke into their home while Uncle R. was away and raped his wife. The rape was very violent, and she later died because of her injuries. Uncle R. walked to Georgia to kill the man who was responsible. The stories did not include the name or race of the man who raped her. It was not clear whether Uncle R. killed more than one man, but there was the certainty that those he did kill deserved it.

Uncle R. was raising a family during the 1930s and '40s. He

cleared new fields of tree stumps (thus the long knives). Long before the use of bulldozers and chainsaws, people in Robeson County relied on men like Uncle R. to come to their farms to move the tree stumps from freshly cut fields. Uncle R. was a functioning alcoholic who managed to keep his family together after the death of his wife. Apparently, his children never suffered because their father could provide for them. It was and still is very important to Lumbee people to be able to keep their family together despite hardships. Uncle R. was also very kind to his nieces and nephews, but my maternal grandmother (Uncle R. was her brother-in-law) would instruct her children to hide the rubbing alcohol and mouthwash whenever Uncle R. came to visit, because she was afraid he would drink it.

If you were an insider, you knew that in the 1930s and '40s and even later, Indian women in Robeson County were raped, but very few of the men (usually whites) were ever arrested or convicted of this crime. There was no justice for the families of women who, like Uncle R.'s wife, died after their assault. Our family stories kept alive the fact that Uncle R. had to seek justice on his own.

Most of the stories about Uncle R. were about the uncle that my mother and her siblings knew as children. Their Uncle R. was a kind-hearted alcoholic because his wife was dead and because he could never get over her. For me, the Uncle R. stories became about getting justice when there was none and about surviving and coping after someone who you thought you could not live without was taken from you. Despite his alcoholism, people hired Uncle R. to do a job that was important to their survival on the farm. He continued to work because he had children to provide for. His alcoholism was his way of coping with the trauma of losing the woman whom he truly loved. Maybe the alcohol was also a way to cope with the fact that he could not stop the attack on his wife from happening because he worked away from home. Uncle R. never remarried.

Uncle R. was my maternal grandfather's brother. I never knew Uncle R. or his children, but I felt as if I had. I heard so many Uncle R. stories over the years that it seemed natural that some Lumbee men just did not suffer fools and that they had their own reasons for doing so. Learning the rest of the story gave me a much deeper respect for my mother and her siblings who kept alive the stories of an uncle that they looked up to as a kind of hero.

Knowledge Is Power

MY LUMBEE ANCESTORS

I am proud of my Lumbee ancestors. They were visionaries. They worked well together to achieve a high level of education for my people. I look at the University of North Carolina at Pembroke and I am just overcome with pride and gratefulness to the people who stood tall, fought, and did not give up. They really worked hard to get education to the Lumbee people. I think back to all the Lumbee people who did not have the opportunity to attend school. I was always impressed with the fact that my mom finished tenth grade. She was a good student, and the community asked her to become a teacher. She taught in Pembroke and Fairmont. She knew math, and I always admired the way she knew math. She always would say that she had the best teacher in the world, Doctor Fuller Lowery.[1] She knew math, and she knew how to teach it.

But, going back to getting education for the Lumbee people: it was a struggle. Every little town in Robeson County had a school system, and the Indian people had no voice on those

1. Mr. Lowery's first name was Doctor.

school boards. They could not vote on the town school boards. They could vote on the school board members for the county, but the white community, which was larger, could vote for city and county boards. They made decisions that were not always helpful to the Lumbee people. My people had to go to Raleigh and lobby. They had never heard of lobbying, but that was what they were doing. They were there to help the people and to get some help for the education of our people. I admire the way they did it. They supported each other. They were strong in their beliefs. They knew what they wanted, they worked hard, and they lobbied. Even though they might not have known that that was what they were doing.

My uncle (who was actually my mother's uncle) went to Raleigh when he was almost a hundred years old. He taught often and shared stories about how they would go to Raleigh to get educational help. He always laughed about the one time when they were going to Raleigh and they went through an area that was covered with water. My friend's father—he was a lot younger than my uncle—was driving. My uncle did not drive, but he owned the car. My uncle had to get out and push the car through the water! He said he pushed it as if it was a log going through the water. But they were going through the water for the people, and they loved doing it.

They were so thrilled when there was money for a building for education. That building was near Pate's, a community northwest of Pembroke. They built the first building there. I understand there were five hundred dollars allocated for the school. Hamilton McMillan was the one who went before the legislature and made their plea for the money. The people gave the land and built the building. Later that school was moved to the present site. The school was established initially to train teachers.

My mother was a teacher without any form of teacher training. She had the knowledge, and she shared that knowledge with the children she worked with. She knew how to take care of children. She knew how to honor their presence in the classroom. And she knew math, and in her very special way, she taught what she knew to the children. She was always thrilled to share those stories with us, and we were thrilled to meet many of her students. I distinctly remember Mr. Marcus Hammonds. He was an elder when I was young, and he would say to me, "Your mother knew math. She taught me math, and she taught me more than math. She taught me how to be a good, upright citizen."

Then there was another person who my mom taught; he had problems with alcohol. He would often come to our house to get "Ms. Godwin" (Godwin was Mom's maiden name). He would say, "I came to get Ms. Godwin to sign my diploma!" My mom would always invite him to our table to eat, and he often spoke of how well my mom could cook. Education was viewed as the ticket out of oppression. Knowledge is power, and that is what my mom and people in my church, First Baptist Church in Pembroke, often said to us. "You stay in school, and you get a degree. There is no one in the world who can take that from you." So that was what I heard. All those things made an impression on me.

MY OWN FAMILY

I wanted to be a teacher, and I entered Pembroke State College (PSC). That was the name of the University of North Carolina at

Pembroke at the time I started school in the fall of 1956. There were approximately six hundred students on campus. I was the only person from my family who attended that school; four of us got degrees, but I was the only person who attended Pembroke State College. I had two sisters who attended Hope Ridge College. One got a degree in accounting; the other got a degree in business. She taught business education in schools. My brother attended Mars Hill College, essentially because he wanted to go to Wake Forest University but did not have the credentials. Our high school did not offer the courses that he needed to enter Wake Forest. He was so devoted to attending Wake Forest that he went to Mars Hill to take prep courses. He eventually entered Wake Forest and graduated in 1958.

Education was very important to my family. I thought about how my grandfather had served on the board of trustees at Pembroke State College. I thought about how my mother had been a teacher without formal training, and here I was, a young woman, eighteen years old, and I was going to get an education. I was going to be a teacher. When I got to Pembroke, I wanted to be a history teacher. I loved history. I loved learning about different things, and I had heard so much about Sherman's March, how close it came to Pembroke. My hero, Henry Berry Lowry, had people from the Union Army to join his gang. All of this was so important to me.

Dr. Herbert H. Todd was my advisor at Pembroke State College. I had taken one of the first courses on history with him. I was committed to working hard in my college courses. I took many history courses because I liked history and I still do.

After I had been in his class for a few weeks, Dr. Todd asked me to remain after class one day, and he said to me, "What do you plan to major in?"

And I said, "Oh, well, I want to be a history teacher because I love history and love learning about it. And I love hearing all the stories."

Dr. Todd said, "Rosa, you have been in my class, and I have been so impressed with your knowledge, with your attention to everything in the class, and how you have participated. I would like for you to become an elementary school teacher. It is so important that we get the children early and that we impress on them how important it is to read, know math, and to know how to express yourself. I would love to ask you to become an elementary school teacher."

At the time, I had not taken education classes because I had wanted to be a history major. Dr. Todd had been such a good advisor, and I did just what he asked of me. I changed my major to elementary education. I never regretted it. I taught fifth grade, and I have taught second grade and third grade. My first class was a third-grade class.

My dad had advised that I would have to go to Pembroke because he had sent three children to college and did not have the money for me to go to another outside school. I adored my brother so much that I had wanted to follow in his tracks. I wanted to go to Mars Hill and then go to Wake Forest simply because Lonnie had gone. I learned to love Pembroke with all my heart and soul. I am so committed to that university and to the opportunities for which our ancestors fought. They literally had to get out and travel miles and miles to fight for our education. Some of them had never traveled outside the county, but they knew how to take that trek to Raleigh. I am so grateful today that they did that. Their effort offered me an opportunity to get a good education.

I felt that by going to Pembroke, I learned much that perhaps I would not have learned at another school. I had teachers who really cared about me. There was Dr. James Ebert, who still lives in Robeson County. He was my biology teacher. He was so good to the students. The thing that impressed me about the teachers was that they embraced the culture and us. I admired that very much. That was a great credit to our people and our culture. One of the things I learned at Pembroke State College was how to appreciate and respect who you are. That meant a lot to me. I have learned to embrace people from other cultures and ethnicities. It started at PSC, and it grew as I worked as a teacher myself.

OVERCOMING PREJUDICE

I had hoped that I would get a job in Robeson County, but I was never offered a job, even though I had four or five interviews. In the interviews, potential employers would never ask what my qualifications were. I would say in an interview, "You have not asked about my qualifications, and I would like to share my qualifications with you." It is important to speak to the makeup of the people interviewing for jobs in the county. At the time, the Robeson County Board of Education was made up of only white people from Robeson County. Indians could not serve on it. For the Indians' benefit, each school had a school committee. Job interviews were held usually by the chairman of that committee. One or two other white people might join the chairman.

At times, the interviews were even held in a person's place of business, whether on someone's farm or the place of business for whichever merchant you would have to appear before. This included the chairman of the school committee and other committee members. Considering these circumstances, I was concerned about why I was never given an opportunity to discuss my qualifications. So, I, a Lumbee woman, was not hired to teach in Robeson County.

The only other interview I did was with the Richmond County school system. At that time, those schools were called Rockingham City schools. I answered an ad in the newspaper and was hired as a teacher in Richmond County, about forty miles from Pembroke. That was my first place of employment in teaching. I was thrilled that I had that job. Before my employment in Richmond County, I had never interacted with people of the Caucasian race very much because I had very little contact with them. I had some prejudices, and I had to work through those thoughts. I did not trust white people. I understood later that it was because I did not know them. I eventually got to know them, and I realized that there were people who I could trust. While working at the Rockingham City schools, I had a mentor. Her name was Ms. Thelma Nicholson. She helped me in every way that she could. Through the years, I always say a little prayer in gratefulness for Ms. Thelma Nicholson and for what she did for me.

When I served on the board of trustees for Pembroke State University, a gentleman from Lumberton was serving with me. His name was John Nicholson. I did not pick up on that name—that is, I did not reference it back to Ms. Thelma Nicholson. And one day he said to me, "Did you teach in Rockingham?"

And I said, "Yes."

He said, "Then you knew my mother, Ms. Thelma Nicholson."

So, we became friends right there on the spot! I have always had an appreciation for the L. J. Bell Elementary School in Rockingham for that reason. I was so green then. I had never interacted with hardly anyone but Indian people. So, by working there, I was taught many lessons. I left that school confident that I could teach school anywhere because of what I learned outside the classroom.

I have traveled a long path, and on that path, I learned how to overcome prejudices. People who say they do not have any prejudices . . . I just think they are wrong. I had prejudices, and I learned how to work through them. Good people from the Caucasian race helped me to do that. Education does not mean that you get it all within the space of four walls. Living in a white community was so strange to me. I learned how to interact with people who were not from my own tribe, people other than relatives living in my home community. The only real contact I had growing up was the fact that I worked in the local general store run by Mr. Russell W. Livermore. I worked four years in the dress shop. I learned a lot there because almost all of my customers were Indian. I worked with two white ladies at the store. I guess I also learned my prejudices in that setting. I was often hurt by my coworkers' remarks. They laughed at Indian people, especially Indian people who were not educated. It was just so hard to listen to those things, but I knew I had to work. So, I just listened and tried to be as loving and as kind as I could to the people I served. That said, they were mostly Indian people.

I also learned from our elders in the different communities

around where I lived, one mile north of Pembroke. Until my time at Livermore's, I had not interacted with too many people except my relatives from other communities in Robeson County. So, I learned a lot about our people just by working in that store. I was humbled. The elders talked a lot about our struggle as Indian people, and they would say it to me very openly, honestly. I learned to love them. I held them in high esteem. Many of them would come to the store to bring items from home and trade them for food or for clothing. The Livermores allowed them to do that. I thought that it was a very good and honorable thing that they permitted people to bring items and exchange them for the food they did not have.

I learned so many things working there. I learned to respect the elders for what they shared with me. They would do it in such a humble way. They taught me to respect others while respecting myself. It is so important to learn to respect others, other views, to respect what they bring to the table. Some of the elders would share with me that they went to the first or second grade only. Some of them shared that they had never been in school, and that touched me so deeply, that they had never had the opportunity to go to school. It really made me appreciate the fact that I could go to school.

WE ARE MAKING HISTORY

Looking back, I am just thrilled that at one point in my life I started thinking about my role as a female, as a mother, as a wife, and then as an educator. I started thinking about women, the women all around me who are the givers of life and who are handed the responsibility of caring for the culture of our people. I like the fact that we are making history. Today will become history that future generations will study. I hope that they will honor our hard work to accomplish great things for all people, not just Indian people. Seeing the tradition and the ceremonies of our people that we have reclaimed, I know that we have also reclaimed the ceremony of education.

As I said, I never taught in Robeson County. I taught in Virginia, Chesapeake at Great Bridge Elementary, in Rockingham, Fayetteville, and finally in Charlotte. I think the greatest time of my life as an educator was when I was coordinator of the Indian Education Program in the Charlotte-Mecklenburg schools. I was so committed to Indian education. I had an opportunity to work with Indian children. Most of them were Lumbee, but I taught many children from other tribes as well. I taught some children from Pine Ridge, some from Navajo country—just several different tribes, but mainly Lumbee.

I am proud of all the kids I worked with. They became good parents. I attended a funeral not long ago, and two of my students were there. They said, "I didn't go to college, Ms. Rosa, but I'm married," and that is honorable, very honorable. I think that to be your child's first educator, you must first be a good parent and be dedicated and devoted to the precepts of parenting, good parenting. I think being a parent is good and honorable in many ways.

One of my students is now the curator of the American Indian Cultural Center and Museum in Oklahoma City. Nancy studied at the Institute of American Indian Art, and I am so proud of her. Jana, a musician and an author, is now internationally known, and I am proud of her. Another of my students in Indian education in Charlotte, a male student, became a nurse. He married a Mohawk woman and lived in upstate New York. He was returning home from work one morning, and he had an accident and lost his life. We honored him in a special ceremony. His wife and children came. As a child, he had a hard time staying in school. I used to go to his home and knock on the door. He would open the door and say, "Oh no! Ms. Rosa has come for me!" and I would take him to school. Later in life, he learned the value of an education. He got a GED and then became a nurse.

Sometimes, it takes some people longer to appreciate education than it does others. I love to look at them like flowers. Not all flowers bloom at the same time. Some bloom early in the spring, and some bloom late in the summer. That is how I viewed the students who did not bloom early. They eventually came into their being and learned to appreciate education as a way of overcoming oppression and all the other things that come with that. Because I was so concerned about all children, Indian children, I did think that.

WOMEN RECLAIMING CEREMONY

I started an organization with women in Charlotte. We had a lovely group of women who came together to reclaim ceremony. We had many of these gatherings, and it was so good for us that the Mint Museum collaborated with our group. Even the director there was so interested in what we were doing that they invited us to come there for our events. To rent that building at the time, people had to pay $1800. We got it free of charge. I am so appreciative to those people at the museum who looked at our culture and understood the historical trauma, what it had done to our people. Sometimes we did not even believe in ourselves. We did not have enough courage to go out for help, but this group of women surely did. They had the courage and the will to stand up and say, Indian children are important.

We went to school for meetings, and sometimes we were worried about going to the school board meetings, only to find out that we would be honored. We were honored at these meetings! They would have us stand up and identify ourselves. This group of women was so impressive. Well, we thought, why not take this initiative statewide? I called out. I had a good relationship with Wake Forest University. The school reached out to us during my brother Lonnie's illness. It was just the right place to birth a new organization, the American Indian Women of Proud Nations. Through Wake Forest University's help, we were able to hold our first conference. We were so powerful that we came on campus in a winter storm! I think we brought the snowstorm with us to the first conference. Despite that storm, I think about a hundred people attended that event. I want to impress this upon our Indian young people; we have always had our friends in the non-Indian community, always.

I remember the library at UNCP was named for one of them, Livermore Library. It was to honor the sister of Mr. Livermore, who owned the general store and most of the businesses in Pembroke. Ms. Mary H. Livermore was someone who worked with the Lumbee people, and we honored her. The board of trustees named the library in her honor. Ms. Livermore was a wonderful woman. Since I grew up in the First Baptist Church of Pembroke, she would often come there and work with the young people. I knew her most of my life. She shared the Gospel with us children. At first, she worked with our inner being. She always honored who we were. At other times, she also brought children into her home, Indian children, to live with her. I want to impress upon Indian young people today that you reach out to those who will honor your spirit, honor your being, honor who you are, and embrace you.

That is one message I would like to leave with our young people: we have always had our friends, and we need to embrace the people who reach out to us. I would love to see more people at our American Indian Women of Proud Nations conference who are not Indian. I would love for non-Indian students to attend the conference. To learn what education has meant to the Lumbee people and not only to the Lumbee people, because Pembroke State College opened its doors to other Indian tribes. There were already students at PSC from other tribes when I was in school there. Evidently, it was in the '50s that PSC's doors opened to other Indians, and then later the doors opened to Caucasians and Blacks. I do not remember Blacks attending PSC when I was there, but there were Caucasian people and Indians from other tribes. Some of my friends in college were not Indian, and that is where I met my husband, Frank.

THE NATIONAL INDIAN EDUCATION ASSOCIATION

In 1978, I joined the National Indian Education Association (NIEA). I was so impressed with this organization's focus on the education of Indian children across the United States. Later, we at the NIEA would also embrace Native Alaskans and Native Hawaiians. I fought to get these people, these other tribes, included. The NIEA was formed in 1969. I am appreciative of the Native people who came together and organized the association. The organization was committed to improve the education of Indian people. It embraced state-recognized Indians. I was so impressed with NIEA that I ran for the board. I was thrilled when I was elected to their national board! That was where I first met Henry Adam. We quickly became friends, because it was evident that we were much older than the other board members were. We learned from the younger members, and we hoped that they would be willing to learn from us. It was a struggle at first, but it soon came around.

Before each meeting, Henry Adam would lead us in prayer and ask the Creator to guide us in our decisions and in all that we did and that the actions we took would be honorable to any of the people involved. The board embraced this philosophy. We worked together to see things happen. Then, as my term ended, I thought that I should work to bring the NIEA conference to North Carolina. I wrote a proposal, sent letters out to all the tribes, and asked for a supporting letter for my proposal. I received one letter from Barry Richardson, who at that time was the chairman of the Haliwa-Saponi people. I put that letter in the packet and sent the proposal. The proposal was reviewed by the full board, and they listened to our ideas.

We even went to the NIEA convention in Reno, Nevada, and presented our application to bring the conference to North Carolina in 2003. We started our presentation with the question, "Where do you want to be in 2003?" Before we got to present the bid, we had to form a committee. We did that. We asked the committee, as many of them as could to go with us to Reno, to present with us. I asked the Greensboro Convention Center if they would host the conference there. Mr. Cap Kelly Howe at the Convention Center worked with us. He even went to Reno to help us present! Needless to say, we won. We had the most votes for having the conference. Then we came back. We organized. Since then, we have been told more than one time that it was the best conference that the NIEA had ever hosted. We really fed them well. We offered all the southern tribal foods, and then we had some southern food items that were not tribal, like banana pudding. We did have a good conference. It is where our American Indian Women of Proud Nations journey began.

In Closing

Contemplating Words of Wisdom
by Our Women Elders

From my mom: People who step on other people on the way to the top always have a hard long fall.

Mom's favorite saying: What goes around comes around.

What do the young people need or want that the elders can say or do to help them?

We reap what we sow.

Reflection Questions

. . . .

PART ONE: MAKE YOURSELF USEFUL, CHILD

In "My Questions for Creator," Madison York openly seeks
from the source of life, the Creator, answers to questions deep
within her spirit. What was Creator thinking when creating
her, especially with what seem to be conflicts between her
appearance and her calling? However, in the poem, Madison
quickly moves from questioning to seeking wisdom to using
these conflicts to serve as a healer. She ends the poem with
the realization that she can be useful as a bridge between the
call from the Creator and her people's call to the Creator. What
questions would you ask the Creator about Creator's thoughts
when you were created and how you are seen in the eyes of Creation? Turning to the quest for wisdom, what help (wisdom) do
you seek to allow you to move forward on your life path? What
is the current calling in your life? How has life prepared you
for this call? If you were to write a poem, letter, or story around
the theme expressed in this poem, to whom would you address
your writing?

In "You Can Help Others Do More Than You Did," Ruth Revels
notes the power of women to act courageously when confronted with unjust social structures. In what ways have social
structures appeared to hinder your life but actually moved you
forward? What roles have you (or are you) currently fulfilling?
Whom are you serving or supporting with these roles? Who

is serving and supporting you to allow you to be useful? Ruth Revels provides a glimpse of those activities that feed her spirit—literature and art. What have you identified that feeds your spirit? How and when do you choose to rely on these with intention? Ruth Revels offered the recording of her life's experiences during the last month of her life. In some ways, the story has become her autobiography. If you were to write a short reflective autobiography of your life to date, how could it help you plan for the future?

In her story "A Firm Foundation to Withstand the Storm of Life," Mary Ann Elliott provides us with a story of a young child's struggle when raised in two different culture groups and in a world that did not support either because of segregation. What experiences have you or your family had in which cultural norms were/are different? Poverty and the struggles for survival pressed Mary Ann Elliott to be useful even as a young child. What do you know from personal experience or study about people in poverty? What forces of reliance do you see in her story and the stories of yourself or others? Mary Ann Elliott frequently encourages us to do our work well and have pride in the work we do. How does pride in one's response to struggles help one to keep moving forward and being useful?

Mary Alice Teets used music as a means of making herself useful. Like many stories in this section, it seems that ways of being useful found the women instead of the women intentionally seeking ways to make themselves useful. These women had gifts that allowed them to be useful. The Creator provides us all with gifts that can be used in community. What gift or gifts have you found in yourself? Who helped you identify the gift? What sacrifices have you made so that you can use the gift(s) in community?

Mary Alice Teets's story also provides us with another side of using our gifts by showing us that her gifts provided her with the opportunity to build relationships, confront barriers, and be a role model. What relationships have you formed by using your gifts? What barriers have you encountered? How has your gift opened you to new horizons beyond what you thought possible?

In "Connecting Memory to a New Reality: An Interview with Cherokee Elder Marie Junaluska," Annette Saunooke Clapsaddle and Marie Junaluska converse in English when reflecting on their ancestral language and Native speakers. For centuries, the English language has absorbed many North American Native words that refer to plants, animals, and Indigenous cultural practices and technological inventions. Numerous tribes have also developed tribally specific dialects in English. What are your thoughts on non-Native languages such as English as a vehicle for Indigenous worldviews today?

Annette Saunooke Clapsaddle states that "A language must live to survive." There are still about 150 Native North American languages from fifty-seven language families spoken today, and there is a promising Native trend toward learning an ancestral Native language as a second language through immersion programs. What do you know about your tribal language(s) and their history? How important is it for you to know and to teach others your language history, past and present? How does this knowledge and your ability to share about your language with others impact you and all whom you might meet?

As is true for Mary Ann Elliott, poverty impacted Barbara Locklear's early life. A family business provided a way forward. Apart from a family business, what additional lessons from your life and experience can you derive that have allowed you to be useful for others? What activities and support did Barbara Locklear rely on to find her own way in life? How can her life serve as a role model for you to do the same? At the end of her story, Barbara Locklear seems surprised that her lifelong dreams of teaching others, producing art, and using her voice to support others have been achieved. What surprises have you found in your own life? How has your willingness to be useful empowered you to achieve these? How do you envision a conversation between Madison York and Barbara Locklear?

Mardella Sunshine Richardson is an example of a young woman who has learned to make herself useful. As is true for the other women in this section, her willingness to seek, to persevere, and to serve others has led to her leadership. Sunshine's story recalls disappointments. What surprises and heartaches propelled her to move through on her journey to make herself useful? Sunshine Richardson made a deliberate decision to move to Pembroke to embrace her culture. However, her experiences were not ideal. They forced her to face some newfound truths. What choices have you made that turned your thinking around and yet presented an opportunity to be useful? Sunshine faced a situation that could have caused her to be dispirited or to retreat from her goals. What reflections do you see in her story that allowed her to gain understanding and move forward? To whom did she turn for help?

Imagine a meeting with Olivia Brown, Ruth Revels, Mary Alice Teets, Mary Ann Elliott, Barbara Locklear, Madison York, and Sunshine Richardson. What actions do you think the group would recommend to each other? As a group, what gifts have their stories given to us?

PART TWO: SPIRIT MEDICINE

Reading MariJo Moore's poem "Some Indian Women," can you recall a time where you felt sun in your eyes, thunder in your throat, and lightning in your hands? Consider writing down this memory with as much detail as you can. If you cannot remember such a time, we invite you to imagine yourself in this manner now. What does it feel like? Write down with as much detail as possible how your body feels infused with sun, thunder, and lightning. What is changing as you work with this image?

Author and life coach Kim Pevia describes a life-changing spiritual experience that leads her from a personal quest for love to a deep sense of shared human loneliness and, from there, to discovering a way to connect people in a spirit of love. Her journey to insight and action is grounded in her complete trust in her intuition, inspiration, and heart. Can you recall a time in your life where you were equally guided by your intuition? What happened, and what were the stages of your journey to insight and a renewed connection to others on a spiritual level? In the present moment, what challenge in your life would be easier if you engaged in the process of listening to your intuition in a beautiful natural setting?

In Daphine Strickland's story "Clan Mother," the deepest time of family crisis brings forth a traditional inner strength to act and to make the best decisions for herself and her family. The author experiences this emergent strength as a Clan Mother. How does the experience of the Clan Mother spirit resonate with you? Do you believe that you can have access to a similar inner strength that is traditional and goes back in time for many generations? Why or why not?

Author Christine Hewlin offers a window into the healing powers of Christian fellowship for American Indian women. Central to her religious "homecoming" was unconditional acceptance and the steadfast support of congregation members. Christine also closely observed how her new religious community "walked the talk." When she discovered a lack of personal integrity among some of the members who first invited her into their Christian circle, she was disappointed. What have been your experiences of religious or spiritual fellowship? If you are a member of a religious or spiritual group, how do you extend a welcome, especially to women who have had difficult life experiences? Is your religious or spiritual group prepared to help women who have experienced domestic violence? If so, how?

Nora Dial-Stanley's poem "Not Anymore" expresses an American Indian woman's grief over the loss of being a free and sovereign woman, warrior, educator, and provider. Expressing and feeling grief is also an important part of healing. As you read the poem, notice the verses that touch on your own grief, and notice the images the poet paints that bring forth a vision of the past that can guide you toward a future. How does your understanding of past and present change as you describe both?

In her essay "Farming Always Brings Us Home," Charlene Hunt connects the moment of discovering her father's dementia to being in the family's garden. Have you had similar experiences with loved ones? For Charlene Hunt, being surrounded by the comfort of farm and garden brought peace and healing of mind as she learned to help her father in new circumstances. How do you make use of being in nature during times of distress and worry?

PART THREE: GETTING JUSTICE WHEN THERE WAS NONE

Gayle Simmons Cushing's poem describes all sorts of Native women. What images of Native women are engraved in your memories? How have those women inspired you? What sorts of women's secrets of the Creation did they share with you?

Ruth Dial Woods was sent on a mission to represent the Lumbee people at Alcatraz. Have you ever been sent on a mission to represent your people? What did it take for you to respond to that responsibility? If you have never had to represent others, what do you think you would do to prepare yourself for such a task?

The Alcatraz occupation was "illegal." It was a protest to bring attention to the plight of American Indian people all over the country. How would you have responded to an action or protest like Alcatraz? What have you done to seek justice for American Indian people? What action would you like to take to bring justice and healing to American Indian people?

Flora Jacobs and Mary Ann Jacobs wrote about their experiences in the UNCP BLM march in June 2020. When have you marched or protested some injustice? If you have never participated in a public protest of some injustice, what cause or injustice might move you to do so?

In Kay Oxendine's article, "I Always Knew I Was Indian," Kay's parents were surprised to learn that Kay did not know that both of her parents were Indian (Haliwa-Saponi Indians). What are you doing to ensure that the children in your life understand their family histories? What aspects of your own family history are the easiest to share, and what are hardest? Do you know the reasons?

Mary Ann Jacobs wrote about a family story in "Uncle R. Never Killed Nobody That Didn't Deserve It." What family stories about segregation or the Jim Crow era were passed down to you? What will you tell your children or the generations that follow you about Jim Crow or segregation? How have lessons about segregation affected you?

Rosa Winfree wrote about how education changed her life. What sort of power has knowledge given you? How did you learn to respect others who were different from you?

Contributors

Cherry Maynor Beasley, PhD, is an enrolled member of the Lumbee Tribe of North Carolina and was raised in Robeson County, North Carolina, in the traditional home of the Lumbee people. She is the Chair and Belk Endowed Professor for Rural and Minority Health at the University of North Carolina at Pembroke, Department of Nursing. Beasley is well known for her work in minority health and rural health both at the state and national levels. She has devoted most of her professional nursing career as a nursing provider, educator, and researcher within the greater Robeson County community.

Olivia Brown was born and raised in western North Carolina on the edge of the Cherokee reservation. She is pursuing a career in medicine and would like to return to her rural home community to help provide health care. In her free time, Olivia enjoys writing, painting, hiking, and spending time with friends and family.

Annette Saunooke Clapsaddle, an enrolled member of the Eastern Band of Cherokee Indians, resides in Qualla, North Carolina, with her husband, Evan, and sons, Ross and Charlie. She holds degrees from Yale University and the College of William and Mary. Her debut novel, *Even As We Breathe*, was released by the University Press of Kentucky in 2020, a finalist for the Weatherford Award, and named one of NPR's Best Books of 2020. Her first novel manuscript, "Going to Water," is winner of the Morning Star Award for Creative Writing from the Native American Literature Symposium (2012) and a finalist for the PEN/Bellwether Prize for Socially Engaged Fiction (2014). Clapsaddle's work has appeared in *YES!* magazine, *Lit Hub*, *Smoky Mountain Living* magazine, *South Writ Large*, and the *Atlantic*. After serving as executive director of the Cherokee Preservation Foundation, Annette returned to teaching at Swain County High School. She is the former co-editor of the *Journal of Cherokee Studies* and serves on the board of trustees for the North Carolina Writers Network. www.asaunookeclapsaddle.com/

Gaye Simmons Cushing was the youngest daughter and self-proclaimed "baby" of the late Clifton I. Simmons and Cattie Jones Simmons. She was born and raised in Sampson County and attended East Carolina Indian School, Clinton High School, and Pembroke State University. The consummate educator, Gaye spent a lifetime learning all she could and imparting that knowledge to children throughout her adopted Robeson County home. Gaye's influence extended beyond the schoolhouse. To many, she was an advocate, ally, confidant, counselor, cheerleader, peacemaker, mentor, protector, and teacher. She was a charismatic storyteller who could craftily spin words to tell a tale while also teaching a valuable lesson.

Nora Dial-Stanley is an enrolled member of the Lumbee Tribe of North Carolina. She has spent the last thirty-seven years as an advocate and a voice for her Native American people by traveling across the country as a Native American storyteller. She has served as a speaker and consultant addressing issues, myths, and educating others about the history and culture of the Indigenous people of this country. She has served on the board of the Guilford Native American Association, the North Carolina Commission of Indian Affairs, the Community Foundation of Greater Greensboro, American Indian Women of Proud Nations, Miss Indian North Carolina Pageant Committee, and the University of North Carolina at Chapel Hill American Indian Center. Nora Dial-Stanley has served as a Native youth advisor in Greensboro for more than thirty-five years. She is currently the advisor for the University of North Carolina at Greensboro (UNCG) Native American Student Association and the UNCG Alpha Pi Omega Sorority. She received the

American Indian Women of Proud Nations Award, was recognized as one of the "Ten Women Who Make a Difference" in Greensboro, and received the UNCG Excellence Award for Advisor of the Year.

Mary Ann Elliott (Tuscarora), honorary PhD, entrepreneur, business owner, philanthropist, mother, grandmother, and great-grandmother, has been instrumental in the founding or funding of eleven firms. From humble beginnings, an eighth-grade education, and becoming a widow at thirty-two, she grew to become known for her expertise in commercial satellite communications supporting the military and intelligence community. She founded Arrowhead Global Solutions in 1991 in the basement of her Maryland townhouse. The firm reached $100 million in annual revenues prior to selling to Caprock Communications in 2007. Elliott's energy and perseverance made her one of the most successful businesspeople in Northern Virginia. In 2009, she received an honorary PhD from the University of North Carolina at Pembroke. Today, she is mainly retired but remains an angel investor and advisor in start-up ventures. Elliott has three biological children— J.R., Sharon, and Dan—and a special son, Paul, and three biological and four step-grandchildren and five great-grandchildren. She resides in Arlington, Virginia.

Christine Hewlin lives in Hollister, North Carolina. She is a Native American of the Haliwa-Saponi tribe. She is married and has four children and four grandchildren. *Bruises of a Battered Woman* is her first book.

Charlene Hunt wears many hats—mother, Luna (grandmother), educator, and speaker of Indigenous truths. She feels honored and privileged to be a member of the Lumbee Tribe of North Carolina. She is proud of her rich and unique culture and tradition and hopes that her story moves her readers in some way. She is also the author of a children's book titled *You Don't Look Indian to Me.*

Flora Jacobs was born in Chicago, Illinois, and lives in North Carolina. She graduated with a certification in Massage Therapy and Bodywork from Robeson Community College. She works as a massage therapist, currently practicing in Fayetteville, North Carolina. She loves spending time with family, friends, and her cat, Preston. Flora Jacobs is an enrolled member of the Lumbee Tribe of North Carolina.

Mary Ann Jacobs, PhD, is an associate professor and chair of American Indian Studies at the University of North Carolina at Pembroke. She teaches courses with a focus on American Indian Studies, American Indian identity, education, and cultural competency. She was previously the director of American Indian Studies at California State University, Long Beach (1990–1996) and an assistant professor of social work at San Diego State University (2005–2007). Dr. Jacobs is the co-editor of one book and the author of several peer-reviewed articles, book sections, and reports dealing with American Indian women, STEM education for American Indian (AI) students, historical trauma, foster care, racial identity, Chicago's AI community, AI lesbians and gays, child welfare policies for Indigenous children, and decolonizing methods. Dr. Jacobs, her husband, and children are enrolled members of the Lumbee Tribe of North Carolina. Dr. Jacobs and her husband attend Mt. Airy Baptist Church in Pembroke.

Marie Junaluska speaks Cherokee fluently and writes the Sequoyah syllabary. Growing up in the Wolftown community of the Qualla Boundary, Marie Junaluska spoke only Cherokee until she attended the Soco Day School at age seven. Since the 1980s, she has taught the Cherokee language to students in Cherokee schools. From 1981 until 1996, she served as the Indian clerk and interpreter for the Tribal Council, and since 1997, she has served as an elected member of the Tribal Council of the Eastern Band of Cherokee Indians, representing the Painttown Community. Junaluska has presented educational programs throughout North Carolina, Tennessee, and Georgia and has worked with Special Collections at Western Carolina University, translating articles in the *Cherokee Phoenix* (published from 1828–1834) from the Cherokee syllabary into English. She has served as a consultant on many projects, including the permanent exhibit at the Museum of the Cherokee Indian, the museum's website, and film projects by Disney Imagineering. She helped the Smithsonian Institution develop a Cherokee Indian exhibit for the National Museum of the American Indian in Washington, D.C.

Barbara Locklear is an enrolled member of the Lumbee Tribe of North Carolina. She and her late husband, John, moved to Charlotte, where they were married in 1962. Locklear enrolled in Charlotte Business College; after graduation, she attended Central Piedmont Community College to further develop her knowledge of business administration. Barbara and John started a home improvement business that is still in operation today. Even though she lives in Charlotte, she and her two sons still call Robeson County home. Barbara says her roots are buried deep in that Robeson County soil. Her sons call it "down home." Locklear served for more than thirty years as a youth educator, public speaker, workshop leader, and professional development instructor for the Metrolina Native American Association and many other institutions across the country as a certified teaching artist and cultural educator.

MariJo Moore, of Cherokee descent, has written more than twenty books and edited and published various anthologies of Indigenous writings. The winner of various literary awards, her essays, poems, artwork, and editorial commentaries have appeared in many magazines, anthologies, newspapers, and online publications. She resides in Asheville, North Carolina. Her publications include *Amid the Chaos* (poems), *Power of the Storm: Indigenous Voices, Visions, and*

Determination; *When Spirits Visit: A Collection of Stories by Indigenous Authors*; *Genocide of the Mind: New Native American Writing*; *Eating Fire, Tasting Blood: An Anthology of the American Indian Holocaust*; and *Birthed from Scorched Hearts: Women Respond to War*. For more information, visit marijomoore.com.

Amelia Kay Richardson Oxendine is an enrolled member of the Haliwa-Saponi tribe. She has been writing since childhood, with her first book written in fifth grade as a school project. Since then, Kay has been published across the United States, Canada, and France. She has become one of the few women emcees at powwows in the United States. Her books include the novels *Storytelling at Marshall's Encampment* and *Satches Lagoon*; a children's book titled *Thunder the Overcomer: The Story of a Long Haired, Gifted Indian Boy* and a *Pow-wow Pocket Guide*. She has also written a series of children's books titled *Here Are My Peeps*, highlighting her grandparents and their lives.

Kim Pevia (Lumbee). Hope Dealer. Native American warrior for social and emotional justice. Alchemist. Honors circles and paradox. Love activator. Challenger. Elder. kimpevia.org

Ruth Revels (Lumbee) was an American Indian activist and educator who became the cofounder and executive director of the Guilford Native American Association (GNAA). Ruth Revels graduated with an English degree in 1958 from Pembroke State College. During her time there, she won the title of Miss Pembroke State in 1956. Ruth Revels grew up in Robeson County, North Carolina, in the 1940s. She experienced a unique three-way segregation between white Americans, African Americans, and American Indians. Revels grew up in a farm family on the outskirts of Pembroke. She married Lonnie Revels, who along with other activists is credited with running Ku Klux Klan members out of Robeson County in 1958. After graduation, Ruth Revels taught at Ragsdale High in Jamestown, North Carolina, for fourteen years, leaving the classroom in 1977. She helped create and run GNAA with the goal to empower and educate the Native American community. Through GNAA, Ruth Revels spoke out against the use of American Indians as high school mascots in the early 2000s. Beginning in 2003, she served as a member of the North Carolina Commission of Indian Affairs. In 2013, the Commission appointed her chairperson, a position she held until her death in 2016. https://en.wikipedia.org/wiki/Ruth_Revels

Mardella Sunshine Richardson is a member of the Lumbee Tribe of North Carolina and a first-generation Italian American. Originally from Philadelphia, Pennsylvania, Sunshine received her Bachelor of Arts in American Indian Studies from the University of North Carolina at Pembroke in 2010. She is currently pursuing her Master of Public Administration at the University of Delaware. As an undergraduate, Sunshine served as the president of the Native American Student Organization and volunteered with the Lumbee Tribe's Youth Services Department and the tribal Boys and Girls Clubs. She also became a member of Alpha Pi Omega Sorority, Inc., the nation's oldest American Indian sorority, and currently serves on the national board. She later returned to her alma mater as an assistant director of undergraduate admissions with an emphasis on American Indian/Alaska Native student recruitment and retention. In November 2013, Sunshine became a federal contractor with Tribal Tech, LLC, to support the Administration for Native Americans as a program specialist and team leader. In April 2019, she transitioned to the Department of Education, Office of Indian Education Contract, as the project manager. Sunshine is a Southern Cloth dancer, beadwork artist, and a member of the Southern Sun Singers drum group. She currently resides in the Washington, D.C., area with her family.

Daphine Locklear Strickland is a member of the Lumbee/Tuscarora tribe. Daphine graduated from Guilford College in 1999 with a bachelor's degree. She was the first Native American to serve on the Greensboro Commission on the Status of Women, the first board of the Legal Aid Foundation, and the Ad Hoc Committee of Greensboro's first Human Relations Commission. She also served on the General Board of Global Ministries for the United Methodist Church and in 1993, received the Christian Woman of Excellence Award, Southern Baptist Convention. In 2012, Daphine was honored with the Drum Major for Service Award and the National Community Service Award by President Barack Obama. She helped found the Guilford Native American Association (GNAA) in 1975 and served on the Lumbee Tribal Constitution Committee prior to the election of the Lumbee Tribal Board. She currently chairs the Southeastern Jurisdictional Native American Ministries.

Mary Alice Pinchbeck Teets (Cree and Lumbee descent) was a career educator, musician, public servant, and lifelong active member of Berea Baptist Church. She was an alumni and active supporter of Pembroke State University (now the University of North Carolina at Pembroke) and received her master of education degree at Lynchburg College in Virginia.

Mary Kim Titla is a Native American publisher, youth advocate, journalist, and former TV reporter, notably for KVOA in Tucson, where she became the first Native American television journalist in Arizona, and later KPNX in Phoenix. She was a 2008 candidate for Arizona's First Congressional District. Mary Kim Titla finished second, garnering 33 percent of the vote. Mary Kim Titla obtained her undergraduate degree from the University of Oklahoma and her master's degree from the Walter Cronkite School of Journalism and Mass Communication at Arizona State University. In November 2006, Mary Kim Titla was inducted into the Cronkite School's Alumni Hall of Fame. Titla now serves as executive director of United National Indian Tribal Youth (UNITY) located in Mesa, Arizona. She is an enrolled member of the San Carlos Apache Tribe. https://en.wikipedia.org/wiki/Mary _Kim_Titla

Ulrike Wiethaus, PhD, is professor emerita at Wake Forest University, where she held a joint appointment as full professor in the Department for the Study of Religions and in the Department of American Ethnic Studies. She was elected as the 2013 Community Solutions Fellow with the Institute for Public Engagement at Wake Forest University and served as a Shively Faculty Fellow from 2010–2012. She received the Donald O. Schoonmaker Faculty Award for Community Service in 2013. As the inaugural director, she has guided the creation of the religion and public engagement concentration in religious studies at Wake Forest University. With Cherry Maynor Beasley and Mary Ann Jacobs, she co-edited *American Indian Women of Proud Nations: Essays on History, Language, and Education* (New York: Peter Lang, 2016). She is the author, editor, and co-editor of numerous scholarly books and has published articles both in the U.S. and Europe.

Rosa Winfree was a proud member of the Lumbee Tribe. She graduated from the University of North Carolina at Pembroke in 1959. Rosa Winfree taught fifth grade at First Ward in Charlotte, North Carolina, and later became the director for the Title IV Indian Education Program for the Charlotte-Mecklenburg School System. In 1979, she earned a master's degree in reading education from Appalachian State University. Rosa Winfree was appointed to the advisory committee of the White House Conference on Indian Education by President George W. Bush in 1991. Her passion for her people, especially women and children, led her to found the nonprofit organization American Indian Women of Proud Nations after her retirement in 1998. Rosa

Winfree was awarded the Order of the Long Leaf Pine for her years of service to her community.

Ruth Dial Woods, PhD, is an American educator and activist. A member of the Lumbee Tribe of North Carolina, she was the first woman to serve as the associate superintendent of the Robeson County Public Schools and to receive an at-large appointment to the University of North Carolina Board of Governors. After teaching in the public school system of Robeson County for twenty-seven years, she joined the faculty at Fayetteville State University. In addition to her work as an educator, Dr. Woods was involved in the civil rights movement, the Women's Liberation Movement, and the American Indian Movement. She has served as a community development consultant for the United States Department of Labor and as a consultant for the Lumbee Tribal Council for administration of tribal programs. The recipient of numerous awards and honors for her work in human rights and education, in 2011, she was inducted into the North Carolina Women's Hall of Fame. https://en.wikipedia.org/wiki/Ruth_Dial_Woods

Madison York (Eastern Band of Cherokee Indians) is from Cherokee, North Carolina, where she lives on the Qualla Boundary with her family. Madison is earning her degree at Western Carolina University and hopes to bring back information to help her tribe.

Acknowledgments

· ·

This book began as a conversation about how stories had been so critical for the planning sessions of the American Indian Women of Proud Nations (AIWPN) conferences. Those sessions always took a long time because we loved hearing and sharing stories about how the planning team members met a particular speaker or what it was like to experience the workshop they had just been to and how much that workshop was needed in our communities. Those stories led us to great keynote speakers and workshop leaders and created lasting friendships. We are thankful to all the women who came together to create the AIWPN conferences and who continue the work of that organization today. Special thanks to all our authors who trusted us with their life histories, stories, and poetry and to their families who also worked with us so that this volume could come into existence.

We are indebted to each other and to the women, families, and children to whom all the American Indian Women of Proud Nations work was dedicated. And finally, a very big thank you to the editors at Blair, who so expertly shepherded our project to publication: Lynn York and Robin Miura and their team members, Ken Williams, Arielle Hebert, Bridgette A. Lacy, and Kelsie Roper.